SHAW: THE STYLE AND THE MAN

SHAW

The Style and the Man

by RICHARD M. OHMANN

Wesleyan University Press
MIDDLETOWN, CONNECTICUT

For my wife, Carol Burke Ohmann

Contents

Acknowledgments

I wish to thank Professors Harry Levin and Reuben Brower of Harvard University, supervisors of my Ph.D. dissertation, who offered very many helpful suggestions at an early stage of this work. Harold C. Martin, more than any single person, encouraged me to take a serious view of style, and his influence on this study, though indirect, is great. Gaynor Bradish first suggested Shaw as a subject for this kind of inquiry.

Finally, I owe a considerable debt to the Society of Fellows of Harvard University, which, through the award of a three-year Junior Fellowship, gave me the time to enlarge my perspective through the study of linguistics.

RICHARD M. OHMANN

Middletown, Connecticut
July 1962

Introduction

 S HAW is one of those writers, like Browne, Johnson, Carlyle,
and James, whose styles make patent special claims for attention. In reading one of these authors we intuitively feel style to
be more than incidentally important: when manner stands out
so persistently and so idiosyncratically it is sensible to ask why.
That "why" is best taken as a request to be shown other characteristics of the writer that make it seem inevitable for him to
have precisely his style and no other. We want an *explanation*,
but the farthest that literary study can go toward giving one is
to say: "This fact about Shaw, and this fact, and this other all
belong together, and they illuminate each other when so regarded. Although they may seem independent, possibly even
contradictory, they make sense together under the rubric of this
or that more inclusive truth about Shaw." Understanding of this
sort is what I shall be looking for in the pages that follow.

   Since American and English criticism have no firm tradition of stylistic analysis, it may be useful for me to say a word at
the outset about method. My treatment of Shaw comprises, first,
an effort to specify the modes of expression he finds most con-

genial in his non-dramatic prose and to judge their semantic import; second, a discussion of his habitual patterns of thought and feeling; and third, a search for lines of connection between rhetoric and conceptual scheme, between style on the one hand and thought or feeling on the other. (This is not an *outline* of the book—all three activities overlap.) In the first and third of these projects I have the field more or less to myself: many critics, to be sure, have talked of Shaw's style, but the comments I have come across are nearly all either cursory or impressionistic, reflecting admiration without dispelling ignorance. Concerning Shaw's thought, by contrast, much useful work has appeared—Eric Bentley's *Bernard Shaw* is a fine example—and I have drawn from this criticism whatever aid I could get. Still, Shaw's ideas and his conceptual grip on experience have come clearer to me through the study of prose techniques, and perhaps others will find that my exposition at least maps familiar territory in new ways.

Clearly this approach assumes a much more crucial role for prose style than it has traditionally been allowed, though poetic style has long counted with critics as part of the meaning and structure of a poem. Elsewhere I have discussed the theory of style in some detail,[1] and I shall not repeat the argument here. But in brief, my position comes to this: The very many decisions that add up to a style are decisions about what to say, as well as how to say it. They reflect the writer's organization of experience, his sense of life, so that the most general of his attitudes and ideas find expression just as characteristically in his style as in his matter, though less overtly. Style, in this view, far from being intellectually peripheral ornament, is what I have called "epistemic choice," and the study of style can lead to insight into the writer's most confirmed epistemic stances. The notion is not revolutionary, nor even on the face of it wildly improbable, but to give it substance requires critical results as well as critical theory. The inherent interest of such results (which are rare in Anglo-American works on prose) is a more general *raison d'être* for this book.

Since I hope to show interesting connections between style and thought, my most frequent procedure is to exhibit a congeries of syntactic usages that Shaw favors particularly, all of which cluster together at some point on a semantic axis; to attempt a formulation of their semantic import; and to outline a group of Shavian ideas or habits of thought that pull the same way. Obviously such an analysis, without adequate documentation of the bare stylistic facts, must lapse into impressionism. With this in mind I have presented evidence of two kinds. First, I have imbedded in my text a rather large collection of quotations from Shaw. The risk that my argument may sometimes lack momentum enough to carry it through the detail is a risk I must run, for without detail the argument falls automatically. My strongest ally in this matter is Shaw himself, whose wit tends to please even when parceled out by the phrase. The second body of evidence on which I rely is contained in the two Appendices. There I have assembled a set of statistical counts designed to contrast Shaw with several other writers in terms of stylistic traits emphasized in my text, and also a short study of Shaw's manuscript revisions. Few readers will want to pore over the tables, but they are there to give assurance when necessary that the linguistic patterns I discover in Shaw's work are not equally the stock in trade of every writer.

Another kind of obstacle to my analysis is the difficulty of preserving a distinction between grammatical structure and meaning. I have in mind sins of this sort: treating classes like abstract and concrete words, evaluate words, causal words, and so on, as stylistic categories. It would clearly be preferable if the only categories used in the actual description of a style were formally defined, grammatical—not semantic. Then the interpretation of style could proceed to meaning without prompting suspicion that the findings had been predetermined by an infiltration of meaning into the initial analysis. There are two reasons for going ahead in spite of this objection. First, we simply do not now have a formally constructed grammar of English that comes close to completeness or rigor. In fact, the whole difficulty with traditional grammar is precisely its incorporating of semantically determined categories. Fortunately this limitation has been realized for several decades, and now that linguists are passing from the stage of theoretical manifestoes into the stage of exhaustive research we can expect the deficiency to be remedied before too long.[2] In the meantime the stylistic critic must make do with what is available. I have learned as much as I could from Charles Carpenter Fries' *The Structure of English* (New York, 1952), James Sledd's *A Short Introduction to English Grammar* (Chicago, 1959), Noam Chomsky's *Syntactic Structures* (The Hague, 1957), and Robert B. Lees' *The Grammar of English Nominalizations* (Part II of the *International Journal of American Linguistics*, Volume 26, Number 3, July, 1960). A second justification for proceeding with the concepts at hand is that categories like "abstract," although they may not survive the overhauling of grammar, in all likelihood correspond roughly to real grammatical distinctions. When the old classes yield to new ones they will yield because of their crudity, not because in any more powerful sense they are wrong. They do have insight to offer—dull tools are better than none.

One more caveat: the authority on which I associate semantic content with grammatical classes is mainly my own. Yet it is certain that purely grammatical distinctions do run parallel to distinctions of meaning, for otherwise there would be no reason whatever for a speaker with something to say to choose one structure over another, one word class over another, and so on. In fact, there would be no reason for a language to *have* a grammar. Moreover, since both my readers and I are speakers of English who daily (though not often consciously) renew our familiarity with the semantic correlates of English grammar, there is small reason to lament the lack of professional sanction for most of the simple correspondences I set up. The reader can quite adequately referee my analyses.

Heavy artillery, all this, to train on Shaw, but his prose merits the most serious treatment. Of course not everything in Shaw's work is admirable, and in the course of this book I have some ungracious things to say both about his style and about his ideas. I think it will nevertheless be evident how highly I regard him, but let me preclude any doubt by saying here that in my estimation Shaw is the most impressive writer of expository English prose in our century. Whatever ponderosity *my* method entails will be well compensated if this book delivers insight into Shaw's method, and his mind.

SHAW: THE STYLE AND THE MAN

I

Modes of Order

Science could stand a cruel and unjust god; for nature
was full of suffering and injustice. But a disorderly god
was impossible.

—Preface to "Back to Methuselah"

A THEORY of the linguist Roman Jakobson offers a convenient approach to the ordering force of Shaw's style. According to
Jakobson[1] the fashioning of speech requires two modes of arrangement: combination and selection.[2] The speaker *combines*
phonemes into words, words into sentences, sentences into discourses. At the same time he *selects* the elements to be com-
bined from groups of possible alternatives that are in part equivalent (words from the same grammatical category, for instance)
and partly different. Normally the two processes get roughly
equal emphasis, but with the pull of personality or culture a
speaker usually gravitates, albeit slightly, either to combination
or to selection. The aphasic often presents an extreme example
of such imbalance; he may rely compulsively on one process and
fail grossly to cope with the other. That is to say, aphasia is lin-
guistically of two types, "similarity disorder" and "contiguity
disorder." The speaker with a similarity disorder can produce
words when the context rather strongly dictates them. He can
finish common ritualistic expressions or clichés, given the im-

petus of syntax, or continue a sentence that someone else has begun for him. He can maintain a flow of words once he is caught up in it. What he cannot easily do is initiate discourse, produce the main subject that will lead into a sequence. Neither can he speak of semantic relationships between words, such as synonymy; he has difficulty saying that A and B are the same thing, or even talking of likenesses between the two. The aphasic with a contiguity disorder, on the other hand, can articulate equivalences—a bachelor is an unmarried man—but is unable to build syntactical structures, conduct ordered discourses, or move from one idea to another that is in some way adjacent. All he can do is deal with similarities.

I mention such extreme disorders, not to hint darkly that Shaw is a pathological case, but merely to suggest that a classification of writers is possible according to which kind of verbal and semantic order they favor. The intellectual bent of the similarity-seeker is quite different from that of the continuity-seeker—compare the sort of mind that finds peace in pigeon-holing with the sort that delights in syllogistic or in narrative. Both methods of dealing with experience are essential to sanity, but it will not be surprising to discover perfectly sane men who stress one or the other, and it will not be surprising to find a writer's preference etched in his style as well as in his thought.

To offer this generalization is not to prove it; it must be filled out and supported in the course of this chapter. But I propose to begin, not by deduction from it, but by looking at some specific facts about Shaw's style.

1. COLLECTIONS OF THINGS

Within the Shavian repertoire there is no more typical connective than "in short." This brusque, let's-get-on-with-it transition caters to Shaw's penchant for rapid movement.[3] It also signals the presence of an equivalence relationship, since its import is that the verbal expression which follows is a brief version of the one or ones that have gone before. Occasionally, to be sure, Shaw pairs up in this way two expressions that are equivalent only in a very loose sense: for example he closes a long paragraph on the evolution of religion with a sentence beginning "In short, there is no question of a new religion, but rather of redistilling the eternal spirit of religion . . ." (Back, lxxiv).[4] This sentence makes explicit a conclusion that has been implicit in the preceding ones; it takes the argument from evidence to inference. But more often "in short" serves as a bridge between mutually substitutable expressions: "George Bernard (Sonny): in short, myself" (SSS, 1). In this apposition all three ways of referring to the same object—Shaw—are so exactly interchangeable that the result is coyness, for "in short" promises the reader an increment of new information, or at least a new formulation, and here that promise is reneged.

The more common and less quaint use of "in short" is to introduce a summative expression that caps a series:

such indulgences as tempers, tantrums, bullyings, sneerings, swearings, kickings: in short, the commoner violences and intemperances of authority. (StJ, 173)

raging and cursing, crying and laughing, asserting his authority with thrasonic ferocity and the next moment blubbering like a child in his wife's lap or snarling like a savage dog at a dauntless and defiant tradesman: in short, behaving himself like an unrestrained human being in a very trying situation . . . (Simp, 85)

by dunderheads, do-nothings, incapable hereditary monarchs, ambitious conquerors, popular speakers and broadcasters, financial and commercial gangs, successful revolutionists who are no rulers or stick-in-the-mud rulers who are no revolutionists: in short, by amateur actors of all sorts clever enough to make themselves the idols of the mob . . . (EPWW, 125)

In each case the final phrase defines the class that has just been partly enumerated; it gives the intension, as it were, of a class whose extension has been exampled. This duplication of class specifications clearly sets up a similarity relationship, with "in short" standing as an equal sign between two verbal expressions. Of course more goes on here than synonymic word play or pleonasm, for the second label somehow yields new understanding of Shaw's subject—to name helps to know. But it is important to see that naming a thing twice means establishing a semantic near-equivalence between the two names, and thus counts as an instance of linguistic similarity-hunting. Notice, by the way, that the first of the three examples above is actually a *triple* equivalence; in it Shaw begins with a general term, "such indulgences as," follows this with a list of the several indulgences, then gives them a second general name. Such triple overlaps are not at all rare; another one (without "in short") starts with "grounds for divorce such as," continues with an extensive list of them, and concludes with a descriptive parenthesis: "(all these are examples from some code actually in force at present)" (Dilemma, 258).

The transitional "in short" invariably acts as a marker of equivalence, and occurs so often in Shaw's prose as to be virtually his signature. Of course the trick of following a series with a covering generality can be turned without the favorite transition, and Shaw does so in various ways. Most commonly the last member of the series subsumes the others, as a general catchall:

they can squeal their complaints, agitate for their pet remedies, move resolutions and votes of confidence or the reverse, draft private bills and call on the Government to adopt and enact them, and criticize the Government to their utmost . . . (EPWW, 52)

incurably hyperpituitary or hyperadrenal or hysteroid or epileptoid or anything but asteroid. (StJ, 16)

monogamy, chastity, temperance, respectability, morality, Christianity, anti-socialism, and a dozen other things that have no necessary connection with marriage. (Dilemma, 185)

a political imbecile, a pompous snob, a vulgar ranter, a conceited self-seeker, or anything else that you dislike . . . (IWG, 391)

Syntax does not indicate the equivalence relationship, since the "ands" and "ors" that introduce the last members suggest parallelism rather than inclusion. But meaning does the job, for each last member is more general than its fellows. The phrase "anything else that you dislike" clearly subsumes and extends the four epithets that precede it.

In other catalogues Shaw saves the covering generality for a new sentence:

trusted and mistrusted, free in respect of religion, sex and color, and limited by age and nationality, place and length of residence. Altogether a queer jumble of precautions against tyranny . . . (EPWW, 35)

You may. . . . You may. . . . You may. . . . These are . . . things that have been done again and again. They are much worse crimes than . . . (IWG, 113–14)

Or the series may be incorporated in a larger equation, usually one built around the verb "to be":

the whole range of Shakespeare's foibles: the snobbishness, the naughtiness, the contempt for tradesmen. . . : all these are the characteristics of Eton and Harrow . . . (Mis, 216)

Langland and Latimer and Sir Thomas More, John Bunyan and George Fox, Goldsmith and Crabbe and Shelley, Carlyle and Ruskin and Morris, with many brave and faithful preachers, in the Churches and out of them . . . were our English prophets. (IWG, 5)

More often than not Shaw allows himself a semantic overlap, in one of these forms, at the end or beginning of a catalogue.

Now the catalogues themselves, as well as the summative devices, are characteristically Shavian.[5] Their amplitude (I have cut several of my examples drastically) and their exuberance suit his penchant for overwhelming the reader with a cascade of evidence or argument or hypothetical example. And though they are often quite effective, Shaw sometimes protracts these catalogues beyond any rhetorical necessity, as if he delights in the form for its own sake. The torrential series is both a persuasive gimmick and a congenial framework for Shaw's high dudgeon. Moreover, at his best he exploits its force without losing any forward momentum. The following sentence is a good example. Through two separate series and one sub-series it runs to ground Paley's famous argument:

And here was a far more wonderful thing than a watch, a man with all his organs ingeniously contrived, cords and levers, girders and kingposts, circulating systems of pipes and valves, dialysing membranes, chemical retorts, carburettors, ventilators, inlets and outlets, telephone transmitters in his ears, light recorders and lenses in his eyes: was it conceivable that this was the work of chance? that no artificer had wrought here, that there was no purpose in this, no design, no guiding intelligence? (Back, xxxviii)

This sentence has enough structural intricacy, enough irony, enough buffoonery, and enough dialectical substance to justify the dilation of its catalogues. But examples are not at all rare in which Shaw presses the device beyond the point of marginal utility:

The lion may lie down with the lamb, or at least cease eating it; but when will the royalist lie down with the republican, the Quaker with the Ritualist, the Deist with the Atheist, the Roman Catholic with the Anglo-Catholic or either of them with the Protestant, the Bergsonian with the Darwinian, the Communist with the Anarchist, the Empire-builder with the Commonwealth idealist, the Jain with the Brahmin, the Moslem with the Hindu, the Shintoist with the Buddhist, the Nudist with the Prudist, etc., etc., etc., etc.? (EPWW, 61-62)

This is late Shaw (1944); the knack of compactness and richness has begun to elude him and he is not above proliferating easy parallelisms for an easy effect. But the slackness of this sentence comes simply from the relaxation of a structure that he favors both early and late. For that reason, and because it fits the pattern of similarity order I have been describing, the Shavian catalogue is worth considering somewhat more analytically.

Even failing the presence of a summary phrase or an "in short," the very construction of a series implies an equivalence relationship among its members. This is most evidently true when the series ends with "and so forth," "and the like," or "etc." (or for that matter, with several boisterous "et ceteras," as above). A continuant of this sort invites the reader to extrapolate the class in the direction pointed by the given portion of the extension, and in order to make his do-it-yourself projection he must first have understood, consciously or not, the *intension* of the

class. He must, that is, have grasped the rubric under which
the members are *alike*. By far the greater part of Shaw's catalogues (and that means very many indeed) are open-ended,
whether or not they conclude with a label or a continuant: such
a series, that is to say, does not exhaust the class it defines, does
not list all the days of the week, but stops with Wednesday.
In so doing it demands that the reader infer similarity, just as
he naturally does when Shaw gives him only the bare title of a
class—ploughman, poet, philosopher, saint (Imm, xvii)—whose
members are supposedly alike.

In fact similarity is invoked merely by the juxtaposition
of several terms in a list. A kind of axiom for interpreting human
artifacts might go, "Things are not placed together without
reason," or "Proximity implies similarity." In prose catalogues
the suggestion of likeness gains a good deal of strength from
the fact that the members share some obvious syntactical characteristics. If they are single words they normally belong to the
same grammatical class, and the syntactic interchangeability of,
say, "hypochondria, melancholia, cowardice, stupidity, cruelty,
muckraking . . ." (StJ, 16) hints at semantic equivalence. It
bears mention here that although nouns are notoriously *not* the
names of just persons, places, things, and concepts, there is
enough truth in the old lie to have kept it alive in the face of
linguists' righteous indignation, enough truth to make us feel
the semantic pull of formal types. Of course the six nouns above
have more in common than grammatical class. They are all abstract, they all refer to human activities or mental conditions,
they all have unfavorable connotations. Similarities in meaning
such as these probably offer the main clues to the notion that
cements a series together. But formal equivalence, I would con-

jecture, is what orients a reader toward similarity in the first place and sets him looking for likenesses. Furthermore, when the members of the series are not so obviously similar in meaning—when, for instance, Shaw includes the concrete "old-fashioned parents" in a series of abstractions (IWG, 195–96)— sameness of grammatical class encourages the reader to dwell on sameness of meaning.

If the units of a series are phrases or clauses, syntax does the same job that word class does for single words:

Roman Catholic Protestants or Christian Jewesses, or undersized giantesses, or brunette blondes, or married maids . . . (IWG, 498)

tall or short, fair or dark, quick or slow, young or getting on in years, teetotallers or beer drinkers . . . (IWG, 76)

the number of irreligious people who go to church, of unmusical people who go to concerts and operas, and of undramatic people who go to the theatre . . . (StJ, 54)

bored by their amusements, humbugged by their doctors, pillaged by their tradesmen . . . (IWG, 51)

Such tight parallelism, through the juxtaposition of identical linguistic frames (grammatical forms) whose slots are filled with different words, clearly signals a collation of meanings. Shaw quite commonly employs this device in his catalogues, even to the point of whole parallel sentences. But still more characteristic of his prose is a looser, more haphazard parallelism, in which only the fact that all the members are introduced by the same connective and contain key words of the same grammatical class underlies their similarity. Generally Shaw is too impatient of artificial stylistic niceties and too concerned with content to make a fetish of euphuistic balance.

His more roughhewn brand of parallelism points up similarity, all the same. Consider this sentence, as an example of
parallelism in the Shavian series:

The result is that powers of destruction that could hardly without
uneasiness be entrusted to infinite wisdom and infinite benevolence
are placed in the hands of romantic schoolboy patriots who, however generous by nature, are by education ignoramuses, dupes,
snobs, and sportsmen to whom fighting is a religion and killing an ac-
complishment; whilst political power, useless under such circumstances except to militarist imperialists in chronic terror of invasion
and subjugation, pompous tufthunting fools, commercial adventurers
to whom the organization by the nation of its own industrial services
would mean checkmate, financial parasites on the money market, and
stupid people who cling to the *status quo* merely because they are
used to it, is obtained by heredity, by simple purchase, by keeping
newspapers and pretending that they are organs of public opinion,
by the wiles of seductive women, and by prostituting ambitious talent to the service of the profiteers, who call the tune because, having
secured all the spare plunder, they alone can afford to pay the piper.
(Back, xvi)

The five-part series beginning with "militarist imperialists" is
bound by the faintest sort of parallelism. Each member has as
its focus a plural noun (referring to people) preceded by one
or more adjectives, but beyond that little matching up of syntactic slots is possible—two of the members even include subordinate clauses. Yet all five are quite clearly linked by their
dependence on "except to." At the end of each phrase syntactic
movement halts and reverses itself like a typewriter carriage,
as the succeeding phrase seeks its grammatical antecedent back
in "except to." Thus the members of the series, however unlike
in internal composition, are rendered equivalent by their rela-

tionship to an inclusive structure. Likewise the other major series in the sentence, but with a difference. There each of the four members begins with the same word, "by," and the re-iterated grammatical peg (it need not have been reiterated) strengthens the sense of syntactic likeness, although the members range in complexity from one word to a complicated system of four clauses. Even in such amorphous parallelism as this, formal similarity pleads the cause of semantic similarity, and witnesses a preference for discourse ordered through equivalence.

The writer who builds a serial structure chooses each successive member with an eye trained on likenesses; he emphasizes the process of selection (to use Jakobson's term) by reiterating linguistic elements that are formally identical and close to each other in meaning. It hardly seems too much to conjecture that these parallelisms take form under an impulse toward similarity.[6]

2. LIKENESSES

In the preface to "Major Barbara" (JBOI, 188), Shaw speaks of "the dramatist, whose business it is to shew the connection between things that seem apart and unrelated in the haphazard order of events in real life." Be that as it may, the laying bare of unexpected connections is crucial to much of this dramatist's non-dramatic writing. The volume *What I Really Wrote About the War* is full of essays such as "Patriotic Indignation" that aim to annihilate the differences between Germany and England and show the two countries' motives to be identical in the large context of capitalistic expansionism, however disparate they seem in the minuscule context of national feeling. Again,

Shaw's antipathy toward doctors rises highest when he considers their claim to being *unlike* other men, to being exempt
from ordinary human fallibility. His socialism is animated by
a sense of the degree to which capitalism soils all things alike:
Trench's bread and Sartorius' come out of the *same* mouths,
Mrs. Warren's motives are the *same* as those of ostensibly re-
spectable businessmen, and Undershaft combats the *same* forces
as does the Salvation Army. Shaw's Marxism is the more ex-
uberant for a pleased discovery that all social malproportion
can be reduced to one set of principles. In all these matters he
looks for simplicity of theory, a single explanation rather than
many parallel ones.

Shaw's knack for effective example belongs to the same
pattern: his ability to see the homely economics of housewifery
as similar to the grand economics of industry provides *The
Intelligent Woman's Guide* with a plenitude of instructive examples. In a poet, this highly tuned awareness of similarity in dis-
similars might have found expression in a penchant for metaphysical trope; in Shaw's prose its outlets are the more dilated
forms of comparison, and a dialectic that is always reaching
into unexpected corners.

Take, for instance, his unscholarly treatment of history.
Eric Bentley points out that Shaw wrote his history plays *before*
reading the history books, trusting his knowledge of human
nature to generate historically accurate plots.[7] The familiar
result is drama that coheres psychologically but pays little
tribute to conventional history, drama in which the characters
talk and act like good twentieth-century Shavians. To quote
Bentley, "Shaw was not interested in the peculiar character of
each period . . . but in indicating what has not changed. . . . The

audience learns that no progress has been made during historical time." [8] The idea that our age has shed the foibles of earlier ones is an illusion, Shaw says:

Go back to the first syllable of recorded time and there you will find your Christian and your Pagan, your yokel and your poet, helot and hero, Don Quixote and Sancho, Tamino and Papageno, Newton and bushman unable to count eleven, all alive and contemporaneous . . . just as you have them today . . . (3PP, 206)

In a letter to Hesketh Pearson, Shaw subscribes to the old belief that "human nature remains largely the same." [9] This refusal to worry about psychological anachronism is important because it betokens a faith in constant laws of motivation and allows a telescoping of time that makes Caesar, Warwick, Napoleon, Burgoyne, and King Charles such admirable moderns. [10] And on rhetoric, temporal compression has the effect of making all events and people equally available for comparison, as if past and present coexist in Shaw's godlike field of vision.

The preface to "Saint Joan" is particularly rich in transtemporal juxtapositions. In the first five pages alone Shaw likens the Maid to Queen Christina of Sweden and the Chevalier D'Eon in her taste for men's dress, to Caesar in pretensions, to Queen Elizabeth in length of life, to Socrates in being misunderstood, to Napoleon, Christ, Herod, Pilate, Annas, and Caiaphas in possessing that superiority which inspires fear, to Mahomet in being both saint and conqueror, and to other dignitaries not specifically named. The whole preface is dotted with comparative locutions like these:

Our credulity is grosser than that of the Middle Ages . . . (39)

[Joan's death] would have no more significance than the Tokyo earthquake, which burnt a great many maidens. (51)

compulsion to take the doctor's prescription . . . is carried to an extent that would have horrified the Inquisition and staggered Archbishop Laud. (39)

The difference between Joan's case and Shakespeare's is . . . (10)

did not apply to her any more than to George Washington. (8–9)

Socrates, Luther, Swedenborg, Blake saw visions and heard voices just as Saint Francis and Saint Joan did. (11)

The proportion of marvel to immediately credible statement in the latest edition of the Encyclopaedia Britannica is enormously greater than in the Bible. (48)

Joan, like Mrs. Eddy . . . (31)

She was much more like Mark Twain than like Peter Cauchon. (30)

A few of these historical leaps seek a difference rather than a likeness, but in either case Shaw's appeal is to the comparative faculty, for contrast is merely a sub-species of comparison. The burden of the whole preface is an attempt to rub some of the patina of romance and ignorance off Joan's image and restore its original brightness through analogy with figures less remote.

Historical cross-reference and other patterns of Shavian comparison are sharply etched in his style. My collection of quotations from "Saint Joan" is not united by a single grammatical common denominator, but it includes several related forms that are favorites of Shaw's. Some of them are worth a closer look.

First, and most obviously, there are the simple "like," "as," and "as if" of simile and analogy, which would scarcely need exampling except for his rather special use of them to compare things[11] that are in many ways quite disparate (italics mine, here and throughout this section):

producing bread until it will fetch nothing, *like* the sunlight, or until it becomes a nuisance, *like* the rain in the summer of 1888. (Essays, 18–19)

To expect him to enjoy another hundred thousand pounds because men like money, is *exactly as if* you were to expect a confectioner's shopboy to enjoy two hours more work a day because boys are fond of sweets. (Essays, 108)

Joan was burnt *just as* dozens of less interesting heretics were burnt in her time. (StJ, 34)

These are the forms that most openly set one thing alongside another to exhibit similarity. Note that the syntax on either side of the comparative fulcrum often supports the sense of congruence:

Joan was burnt
heretics were burnt;
expect him to enjoy . . . because men like money
expect a shopboy to enjoy . . . because boys are fond of sweets.

Other locutions of comparison insist less on exact equivalence, but indicate similarity just the same. There is, for instance, the "as" of equal degree, coupled with an adjective:

quite *as characteristic of* our own age *as of* the Middle Ages. (StJ, 40)

great popes are *as rare and accidental as* great kings. (StJ, 37)

it would be about *as easy* to persuade a bishop's wife to appear in church nude. (Dilemma, 417)

The reader is asked to compare and find similar not two things
but the extent to which two things share a certain quality. Shaw
frequently suggests the same kind of equivalence by using negatives such as "no more_____than_____," the blank being filled
by a variety of forms:

the ordinary private surgery . . . could *no more produce* a complete
modern diagnosis *than* a tinker's budget can produce a ten inch gun
. . . (Delusions, 12)

statesmen are manifestly *no more "captains* of industry" or scientific
politicians *than* our bookmakers are mathematicians. (Mis, 102)

A vegetarian is *not* a person who lives on vegetables, *any more than*
a Catholic is a person who lives on cats. (Delusions, 159)

The second term in each comparison is more obviously absurd
than the first, and therefore carries the first down to its level of
plausibility. Actually, the comparisons sink both terms to equality at zero: for "no more than," read "not at all."

These forms point directly to equivalence relationships,
but it is also possible to play on the similarity dimension indirectly, by pointing to an *in*equality, and Shaw's superlative and
comparative forms belong to the same stylistic cluster as the
locutions of equality. To say that *x* is more blue than *y* (or less
blue than *y*, or more blue than green) or that *x* is the most blue of
all is to focus attention on the tests for congruence, just as much
as to say that *x* is *as* blue as *y*. To say that *x* is the bluest K is
likewise to stress comparison, this time of *x* with the other K's.
Any of these forms, in other words, throws similarity into relief,
whether by raising it or by depressing it. Shaw's use of the comparative and superlative degrees hardly needs documentation,
but a few examples will suggest the variety of possibilities:

[pure alcohol] proved poisonous, maddening, and destructive *be-yond anything* that the *worst* modern bootlegger has ever sold in the *cheapest* speakeasy. (IWG, Stan. Ed., iv)

could not manage a baked potato stand honestly and capably, *much less* a coal mine. (IWG, 122)

It is hard to conceive of anything *more* infuriating . . . (StJ, 44)

[without Archer] Ibsen would be *less* known in England than Swedenborg. (QI, 158)

All the locutions I have been discussing—"like," "as," "as_____ as_____," "more," "most," etc.—abound in Shaw's prose.[12] Their profusion, as well as their often idiosyncratic functioning, is most simply understood in terms of a preference for similarity order.

The evocation of similarity takes still other shapes that are both less classifiable according to form and less clearly associated with comparison. Of Pavlov's experimental procedures Shaw says, "Give me that much latitude and I can prove, by spectrum analysis, that the moon is made of green cheese" (EPWW, 208). Aside from "that much" there are no words here that directly suggest comparison, and yet the sentence proposes an analogy between Shaw and Pavlov, between spectrum analysis and Pavlov's methods, and between Pavlov's results and proof of the moon's cheese content, as well as equating Shaw's hypothetical carelessness in making inferences with Pavlov's supposed laxity. Again, Shaw speaks of "Americans who have made divorce a public institution . . . refusing to stay in the same hotel with a Russian man of genius who has changed wives without the sanction of South Dakota . . ." (JBOI, 234). In this ironic juxtaposition of two conflicting attitudes Shaw compares without any formal signal whatsoever. So, too, his detailing of incongruities: the English object to seeing religion on the stage, but not to having it invoked amidst the carnage of the battlefield or the horror of the gallows (Theatres, II, 22–23). Exposing this absurdity involves comparison, although no "like" or "as" makes it explicit. Such methods are well entrenched in the Shavian stylistic repertory (see Chapter III), but they defy accurate cataloguing.

There does remain at least one classifiable grammatical form that is linked with the comparative mode, though rather loosely: the conditional "would" or "should." That "would" is an ally of "like" and "more" may seem odd, but I think it can be argued. Take this clause: "Under the strain of invasion the French Government in 1792 struck off 4000 heads, mostly on grounds that would not in time of settled peace have provoked any Government to chloroform a dog . . ." (StJ, 41). The meaning will fail of completeness unless the reader understands that the French Government's idea of grounds for murder in 1792 is being contrasted with the hypothetical stand of a peacetime government on the same issue. The comparison here is moderately overt, but even if a conditional sentence mentions only one term of the comparison it usually makes an implicit juxtaposition of an actual state of affairs with one to be imagined, for how can we know what *would* happen without extrapolating from familiar circumstances? When Shaw says that "to forbid us to read newspapers at all would be to maim us mentally" (Dilemma, 425), he offers no contrast to this supposed state of total censorship, but the reader cannot grasp the import of the supposition unless he sees its relevance to the milder form of censorship against which Shaw is arguing.[13] It is a common thing for him to reach out into the realm of the hypothetical for a comparison, and his prose is more sprinkled with "woulds" than that of most writers.[14]

This characteristic locution, along with the others I have noted, is perhaps enough to show how deeply the habit of comparison is imbedded in Shaw's style. What remains is to give meaning to this stylistic fact by placing it against the background of his intellectual profile.

3. LUCK OR CUNNING

I want, first, to insist on the special appropriateness of the word "order" to the patterns of similarity. To make a synonymic identification of two words ("accidentally" means "inadvertently") is to reduce the complexity of the language one jot by adding that much structure to the lexicon. The same gambit may at the same time reduce the complexity of the extra-linguistic world; that is, knowing that G.B.S. is the same person as Bernard Shaw provides a convenient coupling and adds continuity to experience. The learning of "identity categories,"[15] perceptual or conceptual, is for the child a huge step in the process of mastering his environment; he may simplify his behavior a great deal by discovering the thread of continuity in the set of fleeting visual and tactile impressions that represent his mother and another in those that represent his cradle. Such differentiation and identification is essential to the vital economy of a human being.

Equally essential at a later stage of development is the mastery of "equivalence categories,"[16] collections of words or things that are not "the same," but of "the same kind." One may not be able to order his actions so neatly or confidently around the category *furniture* as around the category *Mother*, but the addition of equivalence to identity unquestionably brings a large increase in the conservation of mental energy. The world is so full of a number of things that we should all be as helpless as amoebas without a filing system of categorization. We *order* experience as we order language, by clustering things (or words) along the axis of similarity and difference.

That Shaw's stylistic emphasis on equivalence coincides with a stern, disciplinary attitude toward experience is fairly clear: "The business of a dramatist is to make experience intelligible," not to hold the mirror up to nature, Shaw writes to Pearson.[17] And remember his remark about the dramatist who reveals connections between things that seem separate in the haphazard order of life. One way Shaw reveals connections is through his historical leapfrogging; when he lights on similarities between Joan of Arc and George Washington he reduces, however perversely, the complexity of historical fact. On geographical and anthropological complexity he could also work dazzling condensations. After his world tour in 1932, Pearson asked him if he was impressed by anything he saw: "No. One place is very much like another." "By anybody?" "No. They're all human beings."[18]

And (to turn to style) his frequent use of comparative locutions witnesses a preoccupation with the categorizing of raw data. Saying that one thing is like another, or that it exceeds another in a given attribute, or that it lies at the extreme end of a certain scale, means giving structure to experience by blurring differences and sharpening similarities. Stylistic preferences reflect cognitive preference, so runs my thesis, and if this is so, Shaw's style offers strong evidence of a cognitive system whose crux is similarity and neat, lawful categories. And indeed his stylistic search for order has some recognizable parallels in the most central of his explicit beliefs. His attitudes toward knowledge and discovery, to name the most central, rest on a profound assumption of order.

One use of equivalence categories to a human being is their predictive value; if things are of the same sort they not only look the same, but behave in similar ways, or react in similar ways when acted upon. The category "dangerous intersection" may be useful pragmatically as well as cognitively, for instance. The mind can treat each individual as a member of its type, rather than as a unique specimen, and count on its functioning in already ascertained ways. Within limits, an equivalence category renders the new familiar. Now I have already remarked how Shaw tries to generate accurate history from a few facts, a trick that can be turned only by relying heavily on the premise that like people behave alike, whatever their dates. Likewise he claims always to start a play "from a single fact or incident which strikes me as significant. But one is enough. I never collect authorities nor investigate conditions. I just deduce what happened and why it happened from my flair for human nature."[19] This unscientific disdain for evidence explains his preference for Leonardo over Galileo, Butler over Darwin, inventive theorizers in general over fact-gatherers (PP&R, 73). Thus he admires Frank Harris' extravagantly irresponsible biography of Oscar Wilde because it traps the flavor of its subject, and he advises his own biographer, Henderson, to "consult no documents. Go on your old reading and your knowledge of human nature. . . . What I invent always turns out to be true. What I copy in paraphrases from 'authorities' is invariably wrong."[20]

In pushing toward understanding of things Shaw's fault is more often over-generalization than the opposite—from the failure of his smallpox inoculation to the corruption of medicine, from the success of his own unorthodox upbringing to the inadequacy of all traditional education, and from the *Gemütlichkeit* of his Russian expedition to the superiority of the Russian form of government. He is quick to form categories, and industrious in making experience fit them.

The impulse toward order forms his ideas in more specific ways, too. His social thought, for one thing, plays many variations on the theme of lawfulness. People and institutions are predictable according to their circumstances, Shaw would say, and there is thus a kind of natural law at work in society—or *against* society, rather, since it is a harsh and coercive law, which aids the students of history in their explanations but imposes strict limits on the makers of history. Given its head, history is an enslaver rather than a freer of men; "there is no natural liberty, but only natural law remorselessly enforced" (Essays, 97). The essay from which the quotation comes is called "The Impossibilities of Anarchism": a completely free society would founder, according to Shaw, because it would dissolve man's alliance against inhospitable nature. Similarly, his reservations about democracy stem partly from a conviction that no good can come of such a loose confederation against natural forces. Shaw's natural law is a social version of the second law of thermodynamics. Society tends to run down unless men wind it up, for nature's order is antithetical to human order.

The antidote to this ruthless external law is the counterforce of human institution, human planning. Nature requires that men impose social order or die. She permits communities no freedom "to choose whether they will labor and govern them selves. It is either that or starvation and chaos" (Essays, 97). Mind over chaos—a common Shavian plea. Men must work collectively against chance, which is just another name for natural law. And given the necessity of combatting chance with social organization, a large measure of order is better than a small amount. A partial abdication of social responsibility in favor of chance explains the relative failure of capitalism: its "inconsistencies and contradictions are the accidents of an imperfectly organized society. . . . As social organization progresses and develops . . . conditions now undreamt-of will be attached to our personal activities and liberties" (EPWW, 32). Never one to put individual liberty (that is, license) above a sane disposition of resources, Shaw damns Chesterton for the freedom he would allow people:

They may idle: they may waste; when they have to work they may make fortunes as sweaters by the degradation, starvation, demoralization, criminalization, and tuberculization of their fellow-citizens, or as financial rogues and vagabonds by swindling widows out of their portions, orphans out of their inheritances, and unsuspecting honest men out of their savings. . . . They may contaminate one another with hideous diseases; they may kill us with poisons advertized as elixirs; they may corrupt children by teaching them bloodthirsty idolatries; they may goad nations to war by false witness; they may do a hundred things a thousand times worse than the prisoners in our gaols have done; and yet Mr. Chesterton blames me because I do not want more liberty for them. (PP&R, 108)

In this view the fatal optimism of nineteenth-century capitalism and nineteenth-century liberalism lay in the belief that "a right and just social order was not an artificial and painfully maintained legal edifice, but a spontaneous outcome of the free play of the forces of Nature" (Essays, 37). Artificial law against natural law: much of Shaw's socialism can be understood in terms of this struggle, for he is always on the side of intelligence against the power of blind chance.[21] The twin corollaries of the capitalist faith in chance are, on one side, "the gambling spirit" (Essays, 4), which encourages each man to dwell on his chances of striking it rich, and on the other, the fatalistic belief that "the source of our social misery is [an] eternal well-spring of confusion and evil" (Essays, 28). Nothing could be more antipathetic to Shaw's temper of mind than these two tenets.

If his social thought turns on an axis whose poles are chance and order, so *a fortiori* does his metaphysic of creative evolution. This rather heroic world view, so bizarre as a scientific hypothesis, is reasonable enough as an attitude, a posture, toward the intractable forces of the natural world, and as such is entirely consistent with Shaw's socialism. For here again the arch-enemy is chance, as his crusade against Darwinism strikingly shows. The soundest reason for regarding Shaw's rejection of natural selection as at least one part emotion to one part science is the kind of language he uses in attacking the role that Darwinists assign to chance. He speaks of natural selection's "hideous fatalism . . . a ghastly and damnable reduction of beauty and intelligence, of strength and purpose, of honor and aspiration, to such casually picturesque changes as an avalanche may make in landscape"; at the thought of this system "your heart sinks into a heap of sand within you" (Back, xlii). Darwinian fatalism is an "unbreathable atmosphere," a "blight" (Back, lxiii). Indicative of the curious collaboration of mind and emotion in this position are passages in which Shaw asks

for a "credible and healthy religion" to replace Darwinism
(Back, lxxii)—embracing reason with "credible" and the moral
sense with "healthy"—or in which he frankly speaks of "my intellectual contempt for Neo-Darwinism's blind coarseness and
shallow logic, or my natural abhorrence of its sickening inhu-
manity" (Back, liv)—acknowledging openly the alliance of emotion and intellect in his stand. Throughout the preface to "Back
to Methuselah" his argument allots almost equal weight to
empirical and esthetic considerations, giving one to think that
the wish is for Shaw at least stepfather to the thought.

Certainly nothing could grate upon Shaw's spirit more than
post-Darwinian fatalism, or the mechanistic concept of nature
from which it sprung. Mechanism meant mindless, directionless,
irresponsible motion: disorder, in short.[22] To be sure, it is the
appalling caprice of conventional theology, the "superstition of
a continual capricious disorder in nature, of a lawgiver who was
also a lawbreaker" (Back, xl), that leads to atheism in the first
place. But the pendulum swings too far:

where there had been a god, a cause, a faith that the universe was
ordered however inexplicable by us its order might be, and therefore
a sense of moral responsibility as part of that order, there was now
an utter void. Chaos had come again. (Back, lxv)

The name *natural* selection is ill-chosen, Shaw says, "a blasphemy, possible to many for whom Nature is nothing but a
casual aggregation of inert and dead matter, but eternally impossible to the spirits and souls of the righteous" (Back, xlii).
Darwin's hypothesis might better be called "Unnatural Selection, since nothing is more unnatural than an accident" (Back,
lvi). Shaw's malaise in the presence of either entrenched deity—

the disorderly Noboddady of Christianity or the well-oiled robot of science—leads him to the precarious anthropomorphic compromise of the Life Force, a kind of disembodied Supershaw, hampered neither by the inconsistency of Jehovah nor by the impersonality of materialism.

To see a passion for order as the core of Shaw's epistemology, his socialism, and his creative evolutionism is to oversimplify, for his thinking in these matters turns on a conjunction of major Shavian motifs (some of which I shall discuss in other chapters). But the abhorrence of accident, the drive toward rationality (carried sometimes to the point of irrationality, in the case of the Life Force), and the exalting of organization are too evident to ignore. These quests for order and control constitute a distinct stress in the rhythm of his thought, and one with which the ordering force of his style is altogether consonant.

4. SIMILARITY AND EXAGGERATION

Theorists of perception and cognition, in addition to analyzing the methods by which all perceivers reduce the intricacy of their environment, have paid a good deal of attention to individual variations in perceiving and conceptualizing. The tendency to construct new identity and equivalence categories varies in strength, as does adherence to those already formed. George S. Klein refers to the two incompatible extremes in style of perceiving by the convenient names of *leveling* and *sharpening*.[23] The leveler is more anxious to categorize sensations and less willing to give up a category once he has established it. Red is red, and there's an end on't. He levels (suppresses) differences and emphasizes similarities in the interest of perceptual stability. For him the unique, unclassifiable sensation is particularly offensive, while the sharpener at least tolerates such anomalies, and may actually seek out ambiguity and variability of classification. In the laboratory the leveler is much slower to notice changes in the size of squares that are shown him one at a time, or to recognize figures set against a background designed to obscure them. The sharpener sees color differences that escape the leveler, and more willingly abandons obsolete classifications of pictures whose outlines gradually shade into new forms.

A psychological term for the sharpener's attitude is *concrete;*[24] he stresses the unique and immediate experience, as the abstractor favors the familiar and general. As Klein puts it, for some perceivers reality must remain stable, as they *know* it to be, whereas others conceive it as more variable. The levelers resist distortion, unfamiliar forms, change, disorder—like Shaw they treat reality as constant, orderly, predictable.

Today perception is no longer regarded as a phenomenon to be studied in isolation from other doings of the organism. We hunger for certain types of perceptual experience just as we hunger for certain foods or emotions. Klein has it that an individual "puts perception to use" in the struggle for "equilibrium between two sources of tension, its inner strivings and the demands of reality."[25] The selectivities of our perceptual apparatus "are the means we have for fending off, choosing and admitting stimulation from the welter of the outside world, which, with free entrance, would traumatize and overwhelm us."[26] This formulation is in harmony with the idea that perceptual and conceptual categories work toward the conservation of mental energy.

From the contention that perception serves each organism's particular purposes it is only a short leap to a theory that integrates perception, cognition, and personality, a theory that has won increasing favor under Bruner's leadership. If perception is geared to the perceiver's vital economy, why shouldn't his own pattern of perceptual idiosyncracies be traceable in his personality as well? In support of this hypothesis Else Frenkel-Brunswik finds that prejudiced children tend to be levelers.[27] Their perceptual conservatism is matched by their too-ready categorization of people according to supposed racial character-istics, and a concomitant unwillingness to risk ambiguity or complexity of judgment. They seek an easy conceptual sim-plicity; many subscribe to statements such as "People can be divided into two distinct classes; the weak and the strong," and "There is only one right way to do anything." In general, they jump to conclusions, are impatient of conflict, and cling stub-bornly to preformed systems and categories. When asked to repeat a once-heard story, they distort its unique details in the direction of these favorite categories. Given this cluster of con-ceptual tendencies, it seems a reasonable conjecture that the leveler's linguistic behavior will also fall in line. One would expect him to stress similarity patterns in syntax, as in thinking. In this connection it is interesting to note that Frenkel-Brunswik calls the devices of rigidity and flexibility "formal style ele-ments,"[28] as opposed to the content of the personality.

The part of Shaw's thought and style that I have discussed so far does assign him the character of a leveler, a similarity-seeker, an order-finder. Only one piece of evidence even re-motely suggests the dominance of contiguity order, or as Jakob-son puts it, metonymy: Shaw's catalogues. According to Victor Erlich, the writer who works by contiguity (the realist) offers his reader a stage "cluttered with *realia*,"[29] and the Shavian series sometimes looks like such a clutter. But the resemblance is superficial, for the constituents of these catalogues are explicitly assembled under headings of similarity, whatever links of contiguity may be present. Shaw brings together the members of a series precisely because they are alike. Let him, therefore, be classed with the levelers. What predictive value does this label have? That is, what stylistic and conceptual habits might Shaw be expected to have in addition to those already mentioned? The rest of this chapter is a consideration of one rather decisive answer.

According to Frenkel-Brunswik, the stylistic complex that includes leveling, polarization, rigidity, and so forth, has as another component exaggeration. This is no great surprise; common sense tells us that to place emphasis on polar, all-or-nothing categories is to invite overstatement in many particular instances, since it is not the nature of most things, when they are classified along a given dimension, to lie huddled in groups at the two extremities without any ambiguous cases in no man's land. A person who is "conservative" in the sense outlined above—who insists on conceptual stability and order—may thus seem quite radical in his mode of articulation. Such is the case of the rigid children who think that "there is only one right way to do anything." And such, I think, is Shaw's case.

It needs no stylistic analysis, of course, to prove that he is much more a partisan of hyperbole than of meiosis. He himself calls attention to his habit of exaggeration, treating it as a matter of strategy: "It is always necessary to overstate a case startlingly to make people sit up and listen to it, and to frighten them into acting on it. I do this myself habitually and deliberately" (EP-WW, 49). (An overstatement about overstatement! Note the

word "always.") But Shavian exaggeration cannot be dismissed
as conscious artifice, and hence not a valid epistemic choice. For
one thing, an epistemic choice is hardly the less significant because it is deliberate. Furthermore, even if we agree to accept
overstatement as a mask, we are left with the question of why
Shaw chose that particular mask rather than another. Not, certainly, because it is the only one to "make people sit up and listen," and to "frighten them" into action, for in point of fact
Shaw's rhetoric has probably been least persuasive when it has
been most hyperbolic—the fantastic rantings of the court jester
win laughs but not votes. Shaw is certainly right in saying that he
overstates "habitually," and that habit is not to be explained
away by adding "deliberately."

In dealing with the locutions of comparison, I have already
listed one that can be considered under the heading of exaggeration: the superlative form of adjectives is a clear instance of extreme statement. To be sure, the statement that x is most a of all
K's need not be *untrue*, for there really does exist one building
that is taller than all the rest, one man that is oldest, and so on.
The point is that Shaw's superlatives often *are* overstatements in
the sense of being untrue, and are always overstatements in
the sense of being especially strong, or extreme, or radical
forms of expression. Even if every Shavian statement in the superlative mode were literally true, the presence in his prose of so
many superlatives, and the gusto with which he uses them,
would indicate a preference for exaggeration. A man who likes
to say that Elgar is "the greatest master of instruments in the
world,"[30] that Webb is "the ablest man in England,"[31] and that
"the New Witness is easily the wickedest paper in the world"
(PP&R, 40), is clearly no lover of understatement.

Less obviously, adjectives in the comparative degree generally serve the cause of extreme statement and polarization. The point of using "more," "less," or an "-er" form is to establish a familiar point beyond which lies the thing in question, and the comparison can be of little use in communication unless the familiar point stands toward one end of the scale. That is, one gives information by saying that George is bigger than David, but much more by calling him bigger than Goliath, and the latter sort of comparison occurs much more often. Shaw says that except for Archer "Ibsen would be less known in England than Swedenborg," not less known than Kant; that Falstaff is "coarser than any of the men in our loosest plays" (3PP, xiii), not coarser than Peter Pan. In using the comparative degree a writer usually seeks extremes.

Much the same thing is true of forms like "as____as____." One need go no further than our stock of trite comparisons to clinch the point: as dead as a doornail, as quiet as a mouse, as pure as the driven snow, and so forth. Lifeless though these phrases are, they hold a firm place in casual speech because they offer quick verbal access to the supposed extremes of deadness, purity, quietness, etc.[32] Shaw's more original comparisons point just as surely to extremes:

A life spent in prayer and almsgiving is really as insane as a life spent in cursing and picking pockets . . . (Dilemma, 199)

The notion that any harm could come of so splendid an enlightenment seemed as silly as the notion that atheists would steal all our spoons. (Back, lxiv)

But these points of reference are arbitrarily chosen for emphasis alone; Shaw more often makes a comparison count as both rhet-

oric *and* argument, by enclosing within it a miniature *reductio
ad absurdum*. Thus when he says that voters "have no more experience of capital than a sheep has of a woolen mill" (IWG,
353), the comparison builds on a logical relationship: voters are
to capital as sheep are to woolen mills. Similarly: "an army of
light is no more to be gathered from the human product of nineteenth-century civilization than grapes are to be gathered from
thistles" (Essays, 63). Many of Shaw's analogies play at the same
game:

> To accept a West End manager as an expert in theatres because he
> is an actor is much as if we were to accept the organist of St. Paul's
> Cathedral as an expert on music halls because he is a musician.
> (Dilemma, 416)

All of these equivalence forms represent a reaching out for extremes—what I have been calling exaggeration. Their profusion
in Shaw's prose helps create its peculiar vividness, or, in less
happy moments, its peculiar stridency.

   In addition to these locutions of comparison, which I have
previously used to illustrate Shaw's affection for equivalence
categories, there are other important stylistic patterns that jibe
with his preference for extremities. One particularly common
frame is "so____that____"—on just two pages of *The Intelligent Woman's Guide* (pp. 157–58) these six examples occur:

> It soon became so certain that free Capitalism in drink in England
> would destroy England, that the Government was forced to interfere.
> Spirits can be distilled so cheaply that it is quite possible to make a
> woman "drunk for a penny: dead drunk for twopence" . . .
> had to pay the Government so much money that he could make no
> profit . . .

this made the drink so dear that . . . the working people could not afford to drink as recklessly . . .

it was prohibited in so many States that it became possible to make a Federal law . . .

The benefits . . . were so immediate and so enormous that . . .

It is no coincidence that this locution appeals to Shaw, for it both emphasizes the extremity of some attribute and draws a lawlike connection between the attribute and its consequences. The man who likes his categories tight wants them that way so that he may use just one attribute as a reliable clue to many others. From membership in such a category certain results follow, and the "so_____that_____" pattern gives prominence to this sequence of attribute and effect, as well as to extremity.

Another formal marker of Shavian overstatement that links it with categorization is the high incidence of a certain type of determiner. Determiners are those words which can replace "the" in a linguistic frame.[33] They include the possessive pronouns, the numbers, and, of special interest here, a group of words touching on the relationship between classes and their members: "a," "an," "every," "no," "all," "each," "some," "any," "few," "more," "most," "many," "much." A few are roughly equivalent to the quantifiers of logic, the symbols that indicate whether an expression applies to all x or to at least one x. Here, as often, ordinary language is much richer in distinctions than is logic, and can specify various degrees of fullness or emptiness in its classes.

Naturally these determiners figure prominently in all speech and writing, but one might expect that a writer who, like Shaw, deals both in exaggeration and in neat categories, would favor the more extreme determiners, those that specify either full or empty classes. And indeed, if we count occurrences of these words both as nouns and as determiners, as well as derivatives such as "nobody" and "everything," the frequency is quite impressive. Two pages of Shaw's prose contain the following examples:

everybody	they all
all that he or she had	Nobody
each took	no business
all known to one another	Everybody
all of them	no street lamp
they all	any healthy person (that is, *every*
Each member	healthy person)
Every house	all paid for
have no right	everybody
each family	all we have
they all	do not pay any
every house	at all

(IWG, 13–14)

Many of these all-or-nothing words are unobtrusively buried in the flow of syntax, to be sure, and cannot have deep significance; but in mass [34] they certainly reveal a predisposition toward sharp boundaries, rigid categories, and exaggeration.

Exaggeration, finally, is a common function of adverbs, particularly those that modify adjectives or other adverbs. In fact, this group of words can be distinguished grammatically from those that modify verbs. One modern grammarian separates them entirely from the adverbs, and calls the resulting class "degree words." [35] Their semantic weight is normally one of intensification, of insisting doubly on the force of the adjective modified. This is clearly true of such degree words as "very," "extremely," "so," "most," and "only"; and it is also true in a less obvious way of many others. The modification of "perfunctory" by "intolerably" (War, 257) brings an increment of new information about the attitude of the writer, but mainly it underscores the perfunctoriness. Or consider "really dangerous" and "quite understandable." Shaw's prose is dotted with such intensifiers; any given page yields a significant number of them (italics mine):

too often	*most* impossible
really effective	*thoroughly* planned
so complete	*grotesquely* realistic
extraordinarily sanguine	*revoltingly* incongruous
seriously *enough*	*more* seriously
quite seriously	

(PPU I, xi)

"Grotesquely" and "revoltingly" are the only words in this list whose meanings are not entirely devoted to degree, and even they clearly serve to intensify—realistic to the extent of being grotesque; incongruous to the point of revulsion. The high frequency of degree words,[36] then, is another link in the stylistic chain that unites overstatement, polarization, and equivalence.

When these several locutions of hyperbole are added up, together with some miscellaneous ones, the total[37] is a rather impressive indicator of Shaw's allegiance to exaggeration, and to leveling. At the risk of becoming tedious, I shall include one last gleaning (from thirty lines of Shaw), this time a comprehensive catalogue of words and phrases that clearly suggest degree, extent, limits, extremes, quantity, and the like:

less . . . than	best
rather	every other case
less fuss than	such inconvenience . . . as
either party	ten times over
any two	all laws
most laws	stronger
only people	strongest
no position	avowedly illicit
no career	often
as hard . . . as	as tyrannical
the worst	Even when
all normal people	no such
rather than	negligible
not even	How common
so convincingly	nobody
nothing	various other

(Dilemma, 183–84)

Insignificant though some of these words are, the size of the list suggests the extent to which Shaw's prose moves in an *ambiance* of degree, and especially, of extreme degree. Hardly a sentence goes by without some prodding of the reader into an awareness of extent.

Shaw has probably gathered as much notoriety for his peccadilloes against common sense as for his championing of it. Everyone knows how he fought vaccination long after the flow of evidence had clearly turned against him, how he allowed the useless sadism of a few experimenters to persuade him that vivisection should be totally outlawed, how his admiration of strong men shaded into perverse enthusiasm for Mussolini, Stalin, and Hitler. Is it not possible that such lapses of reason have their source in excessively rigid categorizing? Some osteopaths, radiologists, and other practitioners unlicensed in Shaw's England have effected cures, and many registered doctors have killed their patients: therefore, doctors are frauds and cranks are men of science. Shaw never proffers such reasoning explicitly; the flaws in it are too crude. But it seems likely that his refusal to divorce lost causes long abandoned by less imaginative people is cousin to the leveler's unwillingness to tolerate change, to his passion for tight categories, and to the associated habit of exaggeration.

The drive toward similarity order is on the whole a great Shavian virtue; to "show the connection between things that seem apart and unrelated in the haphazard order of events" is an intellectual goal of the highest respectability and utility, especially for a social critic. But the defect of the virtue is Shaw's testy inflexibility and his accompanying excesses of exaggeration. Perhaps one cannot spend a lifetime cultivating conceptual order—and, importantly, stylistic order—without harvesting, in a bumper crop, at least a few weeds.

II

The Uses of Discontinuity

> There is an indescribable levity—not triviality, mind, but
> levity—something spritelike about the final truth of a mat-
> ter; and this exquisite levity communicates itself to the
> style of a writer who will face the labour of digging down
> to it.
>
> —"Who I Am and What I Think"

1. OF STAGNATION AND CHANGE

THE leveler resists perceptual change, is conservative in his
conceptual categories of equivalence. Yet who ever accused
Shaw of being conservative or resisting change?

In the ripe but far from conservative maturity of his upper
eighties he wrote his last full-scale critique of society, *Everybody's Political What's What?*, a potpourri of his favorite ideas.
There he presses his advocacy of state control over breeding. He
recommends radical abrogation of the individual's right to direct
his child's education, agreeing with William Morris that parents
are the worst people to take care of children. He decries the
"primitive morality" (p. 7) of private land ownership, and scorns
even that leniency which recommends compensation for the
newly depropertied. Government by parliament and the party
system must also be "ruthlessly discarded" (p. 29). And to com-

plete the iconoclasm, Shaw paradoxically contends that universal suffrage must go for democracy to succeed—the people may have congresses in which to make known their wants, but should never be permitted to mis-elect their political masters. An even more severe attack on tradition is Shaw's insistence that England "must get rid of the tradition of heredity altogether" (p. 32), including the right of a man to leave possessions or business to his family. Inequality of income should disappear, too, to take the sting out of class distinctions. The present penal system is intolerable; criminals ought to be freed or killed according to whether they are corrigible, but never punished. And so on. These are proposals, not for petty tinkering, but for a total restructuring of society, for the uprooting of almost every institution that bourgeois morality holds sacred.

Shaw had been uttering comparable heresies for sixty years, ever since Henry George awakened him to the skewness of society as it was. George, as an American, could see that man had *made* ugliness and injustice, and could therefore unmake them —the Englishman, according to Shaw, unimaginatively thinks that the Liverpool slums have existed forever. Shaw welcomed his enlightenment at George's hands, but, his thought once unshackled, went far beyond the single tax in his advocacy of reform. Far from resisting social change, he embraces it almost as an a priori principle: the Life Force cannot reshape the clay of humanity without breaking the mold of humanity's weary institutions.

I do not think the paradox more than a superficial one, though. The mode of order and rigidity that Shaw favors, in style and thought, is similarity order; I have been suggesting that he adheres with more than the usual tenacity to categories of equivalence or likeness. The discarding of human institutions, by contrast, fits more comfortably under the heading of a break in *contiguity*. Temporal change of this sort might easily suit the conceptual appetite of one who does not willingly tolerate disruptions of similarity patterning. There are two ways of seeing historical change as a violation of contiguity order. First, social structure is a matter of functional relations among people and groups of people. To reshuffle it is to alter the juxtaposition of man and man, institution and institution—that is, to change relations of contiguity. Second, and even more metaphorically, a temporal sequence of events may be thought of as a succession of fixed states. One array of the people and things that constitute England is supplanted by another, and these two arrangements are *next to* each other along the dimension of time.[1] If, then, arrangement A differs a great deal from arrangement B, which follows it by only a year, B may be thought of as unusually "far" from A (to preserve the spatial metaphor), and a disruption of normal contiguity relationships has taken place. Thus Shaw's radical desire to uproot and rearrange is perfectly consonant with a preference for similarity order over contiguity order.[2]

A passion for change animates some of his most characteristic positions—the argument for tolerance is an example. Shaw fears that the average man, tyrannical in his ethics, will if permitted "condemn the world to stagnation, which is the penalty of an inflexible morality" (Dilemma, 383). The intellectual bumpkins of the world weigh like an anchor on progress: "Every advance in civilization frightens these honest folk. This is a pity; but if we were to spare their feelings we should never improve the world at all" (Dilemma, 241). The blind urge to follow precedent is anathema to Shaw. Throughout his work there move contemptible characters who do "what was done last time": professors, for instance, who give certificates but do not educate (SSS, 71), and the "industrious dunderhead" who does the routine work of government in between Lenins (Simp, 109). "Do as everybody else does; and never disappoint expectation" is a necessary rule in petty conduct, but in larger matters "it is none the less a law of stagnation and not of evolution" (Delusions, 326). Shaw continues with a statement that is particularly revealing in the light of my thesis: "Mere novelty, change for the sake of change, is needed to make human activity endurable." Elsewhere he says he dreads success and prefers a state of continual *becoming*, with a goal in front and not behind (Terry, 34). To a large extent Shaw's ethic is one of discontinuity, of experimentation, of progress. He conceives the Life Force as conducting research toward the superman in the laboratory of history; to freeze things as they are is to impede this admirable project (Mis, lx).

Since Shaw likes to see himself as right-hand man to the Life Force, it is natural enough that he proclaims himself an agent of change, and rejects attempts by others to derive him from one or another intellectual parent, to explain away his thought as a variation on "what was done last time." Thus he self-righteously protests the critic's pedantic allegation that in his more unconventional ideas he is "echoing Schopenhauer, Nietzsche, Ibsen, Strindberg, Tolstoy, or some other heresiarch in northern or eastern Europe" (JBOI, 207). Though he often modestly admits being the second or third one to have conceived an idea, he is likely to claim that he nonetheless made the discovery independently, and only afterward came with astonishment and delight on his opinions in the works of, say, Ibsen or Nietzsche. When he does acknowledge influence, as with Marx, he lays stress on his own divergence from the master's system. It follows that, having partially disowned these giants as teachers, he much more emphatically denies the influence of his actual childhood teachers; his conviction that he learned nothing in school goes at least some way toward explaining his contempt for conventional education. But he reserves the deepest scorn for the suggestion that he should (or does) make the public his master: to a literary agent who counsels him how to tailor his plays to public taste he blusters, "What do you mean by giving me advice about writing a play with a view to the box-office receipts? I shall continue writing just as I do now for the next ten years. After that we can wallow in the gold poured at our feet by a dramatically regenerated public."[3] He must lead, not follow, the *Zeitgeist*, for originality and independence are dominant motifs in his image of himself.

Shaw's pronouncements on morality align neatly with his intense intellectual waywardness, as well as with his championing of tolerance. Thus he tends to use the very word "morality" as a pejorative, to mean entrenched, sterile tradition. Especially in *The Quintessence of Ibsenism* he makes use of this rather special definition, arguing that immorality is merely conduct "which does not conform to current ideals. All religions begin with a revolt against morality, and perish when morality conquers them" (p. 129). To Ibsen he imputes the view that "there is no golden rule" (p. 133), for conduct must be free to change. Established moral ends never justify the means used to enforce them, and Ibsen's main virtue is to have reminded the public that it must be "always prepared to act immorally" (p. 130). Shaw works this semantic sleight-of-hand—morality is immoral—applying his

own moral standards to the kind of conduct commonly referred
to as "moral." The eloquent treatise against censorship in the
preface to "The Shewing-Up of Blanco Posnet" turns on the
same redefinition:

> Whatever is contrary to established manners and customs is immoral.
> An immoral act or doctrine is not necessarily a sinful one: on the
> contrary, every advance in thought and conduct is by definition im-
> moral until it has converted the majority. For this reason it is of the
> most enormous importance that immorality should be protected
> jealously against the attacks of those who have no standard except
> the standard of custom, and who regard any attack on custom—that
> is, on morals—as an attack on society, on religion, and on virtue.
> (Dilemma, 381)

Shaw's ethic is a relativistic one because of his awareness that
"our notions of exemplary private conduct . . . are continually
passing out of date," and that "the scoundrel of today may be the
saint of tomorrow" (EPWW, 324). Intellectual progress consists
in throwing out the "dirty water" of old ideas as soon as clean
new ones are drawn from the bottomless well (Black Girl, 60).

An ethical attitude that places so much emphasis on freedom from tradition necessarily requires a rebellious independence in thought and conduct. We have noticed how Shaw, like
Nietzsche, sees the great man as one liberated from any allegiance to convention; hence, the explanation of Caesar's greatness
in terms of selfishness and originality (3PP, 211). But originality
is not enough. The intellectual will not merely be magnificently
sui generis; he will turn on society and castigate it, for its own
ultimate good: "no nation can prosper or even continue to exist
without heretics and advocates of shockingly immoral doctrines"
(Dilemma, 385). Shaw defines his own role as gadfly and great

man in terms of attacks on the *status quo* from a position outside
it. In frequent references to himself as a national institution
(sometimes in the third person!) he proffers an image of Shaw
the outrager of bourgeois sensibilities. And in the same vein, he
defends the virulence of his music criticism by saying that "the
critic who accepts existing circumstances loses from that moment all his dynamic quality. He stops the clock" (Music, II,
136). The very heart of his drama criticism is an assault on the
complacent theatre-going public and the dramatists and producers who "live to please" it (Theatres, I, 239). Stopping the
clock, living to please, setting roadblocks to change, acquiescing
in the drift of circumstances: these are deadly sins in the Shavian
theology.

To this unconventionality Shaw owes much of his enormous
popularity. His denunciations of the old social order burned the
ears of the pre-World War I generation, but they stirred the
blood, too, and offered forbidden amusement to the more ad-
venturous Victorians and Edwardians. Even in small literary
matters Shaw delighted contemporaries with his naughtiness.
When he told the Browning Society that their hero talked scientific nonsense and insignificant philosophy, they were scandalized, perhaps, but at the same time they admired his daring.
Likewise the Shelley Society when Shaw assured them that *The
Cenci* was "simply an abomination, an accumulation of hor-
rors,"[4] or announced that "I had joined because, like Shelley, I
was a Socialist, an atheist, and a vegetarian" (Imm, xx). His ir-
reverent treatment of Shakespeare titillated as many as it per-
plexed or annoyed. And what he achieved with these petty literary rampages he also achieved, by and large, with his full-scale
siege of *fin de siècle* intellectual strongholds: almost everyone
attended, and many applauded.

He was still crying the same blasphemies twenty, thirty, forty years later, though, and unconventionality is a garment that can wear thin. People stopped listening. Initially his plays gratified and excited audiences by their flouting of "morality," through the standard Shavian device of assembling on one stage both conventional and heretical characters, to the hilarious discomfiture of the conventional ones. Each play has its slayer (s) of bourgeois dragons, and these stout rascals are among Shaw's most memorable creations—Richard Dudgeon, Jack Tanner, Andrew Undershaft, Caesar, and the lot. Their rattling of society's skeletons makes heady music; but it may have lulled audiences into feeling hypnotized by a truly profound and oracular mind, so that when the spell wore off they were disillusioned to find that some of the surprises in Shavian dialogue are gratuitous, that he not infrequently cultivates outrage for its own sake. And then of course dramatic power deserted Shaw in his last years, so that only a shadow of the *enfant terrible* remained, an ironic reminder of the old heretical greatness.

The principle that I hope to have established here is precisely that Shaw does cultivate outrage—and discontinuity in general—for its own sake. Affection for the new, the unexpected, the sacrilegious, seems to lie at the bottom of much Shavian argument and many Shavian positions. If so, it balances the affinity for conceptual patterns of similarity which I documented in Chapter I. To complete the picture, then, it remains to follow the impulse of discontinuity into Shaw's rhetoric and style.

2. OF INTERRUPTION AND SURPRISE

I have already mentioned the role that surprise plays in Shaw's dramaturgy. It will be profitable to press this point a bit further, by considering a representative fragment of dialogue. It comes from "The Devil's Disciple" (pp. 59–62), one of Shaw's *Three Plays for Puritans,* which takes place in a thoroughly Puritan New England town during the Revolution. Richard Dudgeon, the hero, has previously shown his independence by playing the free-thinking bull in a morose Calvinistic china shop. In the present scene he is Sidney Carton to the town's minister, Anthony Anderson, for whom he has been mistakenly arrested by the British. This heroism is gratuitous, not principled; Richard does it without deliberation, partly because of an attraction to Anderson's wife, Judith. In addition to the general background of Puritanism, the scene has a particular setting in which protocol and tradition are also important—a military trial, before General Burgoyne and a Major Swindon, among others. The trial is a formality, for the British have determined in advance to hang Anderson. Judith is present, but has promised Richard not to interfere or reveal his identity.

SWINDON (*to* RICHARD, *sharply*): Your name, sir?

RICHARD (*affable, but obstinate*): Come: you don't mean to say that you've brought me here without knowing who I am?

SWINDON: As a matter of form, sir, give your name.

RICHARD: As a matter of form then, my name is Anthony Anderson, Presbyterian minister in this town.

BURGOYNE (*interested*): Indeed! Pray, Mr. Anderson, what do you gentlemen believe?

RICHARD: I shall be happy to explain if time is allowed me. I cannot undertake to complete your conversion in less than a fortnight.

SWINDON (*snubbing him*): We are not here to discuss your views.

BURGOYNE (*with an elaborate bow to the unfortunate* SWINDON):
I stand rebuked.

SWINDON (*embarrassed*): Oh, not you, I as——

BURGOYNE: Don't mention it. (*To* RICHARD, *very politely*): Any political views, Mr. Anderson?

RICHARD: I understand that that is just what we are here to find out.

SWINDON (*severely*): Do you mean to deny that you are a rebel?

RICHARD: I am an American, sir.

SWINDON: What do you expect me to think of that speech, Mr. Anderson?

RICHARD: I never expect a soldier to think, sir. (BURGOYNE *is boundlessly delighted by this retort, which almost reconciles him to the loss of America.*)

SWINDON (*whitening with anger*): I advise you not to be insolent, prisoner.

RICHARD: You can't help yourself, General. When you make up your mind to hang a man, you put yourself at a disadvantage with him. Why should I be civil to you? I may as well be hanged for a sheep as a lamb.

SWINDON: You have no right to assume that the court has made up its mind without a fair trial. And you will please not address me as General. I am Major Swindon.

RICHARD: A thousand pardons. I thought I had the honor of addressing Gentlemanly Johnny.

(*Sensation among the officers. The* SERGEANT *has a narrow escape from a guffaw.*)

BURGOYNE (*with extreme suavity*): I believe I am Gentlemanly Johnny, sir, at your service. My more intimate friends call me General Burgoyne. (RICHARD *bows with perfect politeness.*) You will understand, sir, I hope, since you seem to be a gentleman and a man of some spirit in spite of your calling, that if we should have the misfortune to hang you, we shall do so as a mere matter of political necessity and military duty, without any personal ill-feeling.

RICHARD: Oh, quite so. That makes all the difference in the world, of course.

(*They all smile in spite of themselves; and some of the younger officers burst out laughing.*)

JUDITH (*her dread and horror deepening at every one of these jests and compliments*): How *can* you?

RICHARD: You promised to be silent.

BURGOYNE (*to* JUDITH, *with studied courtesy*): Believe me, Madam, your husband is placing us under the greatest obligation by taking this very disagreeable business so thoroughly in the spirit of a gentleman. Sergeant: give Mr. Anderson a chair. (*The* SERGEANT *does so.* RICHARD *sits down.*) Now, Major Swindon: we are waiting for you.

SWINDON: You are aware, I presume, Mr. Anderson, of your obligations as a subject of His Majesty King George the Third.

RICHARD: I am aware, sir, that His Majesty King George the Third is about to hang me because I object to Lord North's robbing me.

SWINDON: That is a treasonable speech, sir.

RICHARD (*briefly*): Yes. I meant it to be.

BURGOYNE (*strongly deprecating this line of defence, but still polite*): Don't you think, Mr. Anderson, that this is rather—if you will excuse the word—a vulgar line to take? Why should you cry out robbery because of a stamp duty and a tea duty and so forth? After all, it is the essence of your position as a gentleman that you pay with a good grace.

RICHARD: It is not the money, General. But to be swindled by a pig-headed lunatic like King George—

SWINDON (*scandalized*): Chut, sir—silence!

SERGEANT (*in stentorian tones, greatly shocked*): Silence!

BURGOYNE (*unruffled*): Ah, that is another point of view. My position does not allow of my going into that, except in private. But (*shrugging his shoulders*) of course, Mr. Anderson, if you are determined to be hanged (JUDITH *flinches.*) there's nothing more to be said. An unusual taste! however (*with a final shrug*)—!

SWINDON (*to* BURGOYNE): Shall we call witnesses?

RICHARD: What need is there of witnesses? If the townspeople here had listened to me, you would have found the streets barricaded, the houses loopholed, and the people in arms to hold the town against you to the last man. But you arrived, unfortunately, before we had got out of the talking stage; and then it was too late.

SWINDON (*severely*): Well, sir, we shall teach you and your townspeople a lesson they will not forget. Have you anything more to say?

RICHARD: I think you might have the decency to treat me as a prisoner of war, and shoot me like a man instead of hanging me like a dog.

BURGOYNE (*sympathetically*): Now there, Mr. Anderson, you talk like a civilian, if you will excuse my saying so. Have you any idea of the average marksmanship of the army of His Majesty King George the Third? If we make you up a firing party, what will happen? Half of them will miss you: the rest will make a mess of the business and leave you to the provo-marshal's pistol. Whereas we can hang you in a perfectly workmanlike and agreeable way. (*kindly*): Let me persuade you to be hanged, Mr. Anderson?

JUDITH (*sick with horror*): My God!

Swindon, and to a lesser extent Judith, represent convention; he is the upholder of protocol, and both of them display reliably ordinary emotional responses. Thus they serve as sounding boards for the ruthless oddity of Richard and Burgoyne, the two originals. The proceedings get derailed at the very beginning from the track of legal predictability when Richard calls into question the reasonableness of asking a man's name *after* arresting him and bringing him to trial. He then underlines his role as defier of conventions by ironically echoing Swindon's "As a matter of form." Burgoyne's remark shows that he too rejects the part assigned to him by protocol; there is a war on, and "Anderson" is a rebel on trial for treason, but the General imperturbably treats him as a fellow gentleman, and more important, a fellow human being. Burgoyne's interest, like his elaborate politeness, is quite genuine. But Richard's answer is a good-natured reminder that he is there to be hanged, not to proselytize; thus already he has mocked both Swindon's preoccupation with formality and the General's attempt to gloss over mortal enmities inherent in the situation.

The pattern continues. Richard makes a flippant retort about the mental capacity of soldiers, and answers Swindon's angry warning by pointing out, rightly, that to condemn a man to death is to relinquish control over his manners. Swindon takes offense at this cynicism, but Burgoyne merely seems afraid that it reflects unfavorably on his hospitality (he has refrained from taking any offense at all, even at the impertinence of being called "Gentlemanly Johnny" to his face). Now he is the one to reduce the proprieties to absurdity, by talking as if hanging were a minor unpleasantness between two gentlemen. Richard collaborates in the gambit, and this time Judith speaks for shocked conventionality. Richard goes on to boast of his frustrated intention to defy the British, and, worse yet, he libels King George. Again, Burgoyne declines the invitation to take offense, urbanely remarking Richard's "unusual taste" for being hanged. The final reversal of respectability is the General's argument for the superiority of gallows to firing squad. Throughout the excerpt, stock responses take a relentless beating from Richard and Burgoyne, who horrify Judith by treating death in a perfectly offhand manner, and scandalize Swindon by their disdain for protocol. The contrast between their attitudes and the gravity of the situation gives the scene its irony, and Richard's sniping at the hypocrisy of social forms gives it vigor (note his tongue-in-cheek use of "sir" in addressing Swindon). The play has been belittled as a "conventional melodrama,"[5] but though it is not on the surface a drama of ideas, scenes such as the one I have been discussing imply serious criticism of sham morality, and constitute reason enough for taking "The Devil's Disciple" as vintage Shaw.

If the trial scene exploits shock in its opposition of commonplace and heresy, it does so almost as strikingly in its dramatic style. Ordinary street-corner or coffee-cup conversation does not offer many surprises. A careful listener will be able to predict fairly accurately, not the exact words of a polite response, but its general tenor, and sometimes the initial words; for conversation, like individual discourse, is partly a matter of sequence. Each remark is much more likely to be succeeded by some than by others. The less a conversation follows paths of low resistance, the less "ordinary" it is. By this standard, clearly, the talk in Shaw's plays is quite bizarre. Instead of running on an established track, each participant pushing it along one crosstie further, it constantly shifts direction, often to the point of argumentativeness. My excerpt from the trial scene is not an argument, yet, out of thirty-nine speeches about twenty-eight

involve shifts in direction, are contentious rather than co-oper-
ative. In a Shaw play it is always less common for a speaker to
acquiesce in the substance or tone of his interlocutor's speech
than for him to contest a point, qualify, accuse, or even vilify.
(Shavian speeches commonly begin with rejoiners like "nonsense" or "stuff.") Many of the initial locutions here betoken
opposition of wills in one way or another: "We are not . . ."
"Oh, not you . . ." "I advise you not . . ." "You have no right . . ."
"How *can* you?" "Don't you think . . ." "It is not . . ." "Chut,
sir, . . ." "Silence!" "My God!" The high proportion of negatives
and interrogatives is a sign that the course of a Shavian discussion never does run smooth.[6] A disregard for linguistic expectations runs parallel to Shaw's violations of the other con-
tinuities, traditional etiquette, protocol, morality.

In the non-dramatic prose, too, surprise is a major principle of construction. I refer to discontinuity both with social
convention and with syntactic expectations; nor are the two
really separate, for one's expectation as to what will come next
in a bit of discourse hangs on semantic considerations as well
as syntactic ones, and part of one's semantic expectation is that
morality will not be too blatantly disregarded. Nobody used to
expect any given word in a novel to be followed by an obscenity,
because ungentle reference in print to excrement or procreation
was thought improper. The outlaw status of obscenities com-
bined with their infrequency of occurrence to make them doubly
shocking when a writer did use one. Expectations that depend
on propriety of meaning overlap with those that depend on
continuity of the discourse; yet some expectations are clearly
more semantic than others, and with them I propose to begin,
working gradually toward the other end of the scale.

For one thing, I can dismiss them fairly quickly: everyone knows without being shown that Shaw flippantly ignores the sanctions and taboos of bourgeois culture. That he stood in merriment over his mother's fresh ashes is a symbolic fact. But consider one set of examples, which has to do with Christianity. Society expects, if not credence of the established religion, at least respect for the personages, icons, and private words of that religion. But Shaw, as he put it, "was a Freethinker before I knew how to think,"[7] and his voice refuses to grow hushed with every mention of Christianity. He speaks of the "extermination of Jesus Christ," for which there was a "strong case" because he seemed "a heretic and an impostor . . . a rioter and a Communist . . . a dangerous madman" (Too True, 153). In Russia, he says elsewhere, "the Church is called the Communist Party" (Too True, 17). Pilate is "a trifle above the average of colonial governors" (Too True, 166). As usual, Shaw is obliterating differences and stressing similarities, and this process of leveling can take surprise to the border of blasphemy when the subject is Christianity.

The whole preface to "Androcles and the Lion" is an exercise in viewing Christianity through untinted glasses, as some of the chapter headings suggest: "Jesus as Biologist," "Was Jesus a Coward?," "Matthew Imputes Bigotry to Jesus." Placing the name "Jesus" in such linguistic contexts reduces him to parity with other mortal products of the Life Force. Shaw himself points out that

if you venture to wonder how Christ would have looked if he had shaved and had his hair cut, or what size in shoes he took, or whether he swore when he stood on a nail in the carpenter's shop, or could not button his robe when he was in a hurry . . . you will produce an

extraordinary dismay and horror among the iconolaters. You will have
made . . . the statue descend from its pedestal . . . (And, 49)

A large amount of verbal pedestal-removing goes on in this
preface. Luke's Gospel is like an "adaptation of the unromantic
Matthew to the Parisian stage" (p. 35). Theologians have "conceived God as a magnate keeping men and angels as Lord
Rothschild keeps buffaloes and emus at Tring" (p. 62). Luther
"abolished the charge for admission to heaven" (p. 15). "The
crucifixion was a complete political success" (p. 73). The surprise that comes with each of these verbal juxtapositions is, I
think, largely moral (and must certainly have been so when
Shaw was writing). William Irvine has it that Shaw "nearly
always shocks and dumbfounds in such a way as to provoke
thought."[8] Perhaps; but it is inefficient and ultimately uncon-
vincing to account for his cavalier handling of society's holy
things solely by appealing to utility. Surely he cultivates irreverence for its own sake, too. In print he has confessed to a
"desperate temptation" to bring his high and tragic scenes
tumbling down in anticlimax, in "some absurd joke."[9] The same
irresistible temptation seems implicit in his chronic irreverence.

The penchant for flouting expectations spills over easily
enough into the device of paradox. Although Shaw is no Chesterton whose thought moves from one paradox to the next without touching ground, his thought does come to rest in them
incidentally, as a result of his deep sense of the oddness of
things. A typical Shavian paradox runs like this: America is "a
country where every citizen is free to suppress liberty" (QI,
298). In a reasonable world freedom would not lead to suppression of liberty, but it is precisely the world's *un*reasonable-

ness that elicits these paradoxes. Conduct is inconsistent. The
businessman "goes on Sunday to the church with the regularity
of the village blacksmith, there to renounce and abjure before
his God the line of conduct which he intends to pursue with all
his might during the following week" (Essays, 7). As this anom-
aly suggests, the twisted and knotted social system—capitalism
—is a rich mine for Shavian paradox, so many affronts does it
offer to common sense. Thus Jack Tanner's "Maxims for Revolutionists" (at the end of "Man and Superman"), since they
deal mainly with society and human conduct, are strung together on the thread of paradox:

Liberty means responsibility. That is why most men dread it.

The golden rule is that there are no golden rules.

Masters and servants are both tyrannical; but the masters are the
more dependent of the two.

Decency is Indecency's Conspiracy of Silence.

Every genuinely benevolent person loathes almsgiving and mendic-
ity.

The conversion of a savage to Christianity is the conversion of Christianity to savagery.

In a world so irrationally structured and yet so complacent as
that of the Victorian bourgeoisie, a free-roving mind like Shaw's
finds much incongruity, both serious and comical. The truth
about a matter is spritelike (to continue with the epigraph of
this chapter): "It is the half-truth which is congruous, heavy,
serious, and suggestive of a middle-aged or elderly philosopher.
The whole truth is often the first thing that comes into the head
of a fool or a child."[10] The whole truth is often queer; hence

paradox. Notice that paradox *is* a matter of truth, that is, of semantic surprise, not one that can easily be analyzed in formal terms. But, like any discontinuity in a discourse, it is also a stylistic trait.

A look back at the six maxims quoted above will show that three of them take the form, more or less, of definitions. Now definition, obviously, has a place among the stylistic patterns of similarity, for it involves equivalence between two verbal expressions. There is a substantial difference, however, between the typical dictionary definition and the paradoxical Shavian one. The dictionary sets out to pair expressions that are equivalent in ordinary usage, but Shaw's definitions smack more of the levity of truth than of common usage. Many are quite as perverse as Jack Tanner's. For example:

What is called "an independence," meaning an abject and total dependence on the labor of others. (Essays, 110)

blasphemy and sedition (meaning the truth about Church and State). (Back, xiv)

the quaint phenomenon known as the Old School Ties, meaning the government of modern States by Cabinets in which the outlooks on society of Noah and Samuel, of William the Conqueror and Henry the Seventh, of Cromwell and Tom Paine, of Adam Smith and Robert Owen, of Jesus and Charles Darwin, are all jumbled up in incredible confusion. (EPWW, 4)

These are not so much definitions—elucidations of accepted meaning—as *re*definitions—rejections of accepted meaning. The ground for rejection is usually the inapplicability of society's polite names to the facts they describe. The word "meaning," which Shaw uses to introduce his *definiens,* has here a cynical cast, for it presages exposure of hypocrisy.

When Shaw does not use the word "meaning" as an equals sign in his redefinitions, he sometimes builds them around the copula, but more often he houses them in appositions and appositionlike forms. Hence, I think, their peculiar effectiveness as devices of surprise, for such grammatical pairing brings the two supposedly equivalent elements into the tightest possible juxtaposition, and throws their actual disparity into bold relief. In appositions one expects merely uncontroversial, clarifying remarks, not semantic bombshells. Thus Shaw gets particular force behind his satirical jab at doctors by putting it modestly in parentheses: "Doctors who are up-to-date (say .00005 per cent of all the registered practitioners, and 20 per cent of the unregistered ones)" (Back, xiv). The surprise reversal can be almost as offhand when introduced by "that is" (Shakespeare knew "as much Latin and Greek as most university passmen retain: that is, for practical purposes, none at all"—StJ, 10), or by "in short" (see Chapter I). Occasionally Shaw reverses the order of the equivalence, giving the true phrase first and the false one second: "handsome, wholesome, simple, and cool, or, as a rich English manufacturer would express it, poor, bare, ridiculous and unhomely" (3PP, 118). But the result is the same whatever the order: a capricious disrupting of normal semantic continuity. Of the modes of surprise I have examined so far, this is the first that can be conceived as a play on a particular syntactic form; Shaw is exploiting apposition for the purposes of discontinuity, and this fact is reflected in the unusual number of appositional forms scattered through his prose.[11]

Chapter I affords several other examples of Shavian stylistic forms that can answer to the demands of surprise as well as those of conceptual leveling. When a writer brings two or more words into syntactic parity, at least some incongruity is implied, since the "things" that are listed together to stress their similarity will be *different* as well as similar. Remember Shaw's avowed purpose of showing connections between things that ordinarily seem unrelated. But he often seeks out more than routine oddity. Thus when he makes Latimer, More, and Bunyan syntactic bedfellows with Shelley (IWG, 5), or Dickens and Ruskin with Hitler and Mussolini (EPWW, 29), or Confucius, Jesus, and Luther with Marx, Trotsky, and Stalin (EPWW, 45), he is courting shock. The same is true, less spectacularly, when he calls Nordau a "born theorist, reasoner, and busybody" (QI, 326), dissipating the movement of the series in an incongruous final member, or when he talks of a man's prospects, "professional, mercantile, political, and matrimonial" (Essays, 112), snatching the halo from marriage by classing it with matters supposedly more humdrum. This characteristic linking of disparate things does not, of course, require a whole series as field of operation; even a pair of words or phrases can suggest incongruity, as when Shaw speaks of the "stultification and damnation" that ensued from Darwinism (Back, li) or of Joan as "the most notable Warrior Saint in the Christian calendar, and the queerest fish among the eccentric worthies of the Middle Ages" (StJ, 3). All of these Shavianisms couple syntactic similarity with semantic disparity; they count as documentation, therefore, of Shaw's affection for discontinuity.

In a host of less major ways Shaw detours his prose from the path of least resistance. Bonamy Dobree has praised him for avoiding clichés;[12] as a matter of fact one of Shaw's favorite tricks is to take a cliché and reshape it to his own use. Thus he gives us:

suffers a Lake change [at Geneva] (War, 419)

Tom, Dick and Harriet (EPWW, 297)

the long run (which nowadays is a very short run) (IWG, 424)

a *diabolus ex machina* (StJ, 51)

a Man Question (IWG, 197)

the Inge In Itself (PP&R, 165)

"The Revolutionist's Handbook" is full of uprooted proverbs such as "The love of economy is the root of all virtue" and "Do not do unto others as you would that they should do unto you. Their tastes may not be the same." Shaw mentions elsewhere "an irresistible force which met an immovable obstacle and developed the heat that consumed poor Joan" (StJ, 31). At the beginning of such a tired old saw the reader's inner eye glazes over, closed to meaning until the well-known words have run their inevitable course. But Shaw resuscitates the dead image by following out its implications and by working innovations on its verbal formula.

Again, although he is not especially notable as a maker of metaphor, he does often seize on a ready-made one and expand it. Thus a casually mentioned "gulf of despair" (Back, xliii) returns a few lines later to "swallow up Paley, and the Disorderly designer"; in the next sentence it turns into a seemingly "convenient grave," which was actually a "bottomless pit" around which Darwin "left a path," though his followers dug theirs right through the middle. Such verbal dallying, both with clichés and with stock metaphors, represents a willingness to violate the ordinary expectations of plodding continuity. It is not, to be sure, a private Shavian trait, but a characteristic of many good writers.

Even an adjective-noun or adverb-adjective collocation can carry a freight of Shavian unpredictability; take these examples from the preface to "Saint Joan": Joan was "judicially burnt" (p. 3); the idea of legal insanity is "a medico-legal superstition" (p. 11); Joan is "mentally excessive" (p. 13). Burning is not generally thought of as judicial, medicine and law are not ordinarily called superstitions, and people are more often said to be mentally defective than mentally excessive. Nor does Shaw's flair for stylistic surprise and innovation admit as a limit the two-word phrase. He actually plays tricks with the most minute composite units of all, words. For a purpose or for fun he is constantly making up new words or deforming old ones. Hence, a Shavian glossary would include such free applications of affixes as "fashify" (to make fascist), "Christianly," "infatuatedly," "unassault," "Jerichowise," and "deruffianize"; and such original combinations as "illusionproof," "burglarious," "supertramps," "softships" (as opposed to hardships), "Bardolatry" (worship of Shakespeare instead of Shaw), Bardicide (what Sir Henry Irving practiced), "Listerious" and "Listerics" (tomfoolery over antiseptic surgery), "Potsdamnation" (Prussian militarism), "downstart" (what Shaw claims to be), and "Crosstianity"—the last two being particular favorites of his. Word play of this sort illustrates as well as anything else his refusal to be bound by the most ordinary sequences of ordinary language, those of morphemes within words. Disruption is one of his trademarks.

Word formation is a matter of microstylistics (if I may coin a word myself). A macrostylistic study of Shaw would also reveal many signs of discontinuity. I have already analyzed the rhetoric of a dramatic scene, emphasizing its reversals and turnings. The point could have been made much more spectacularly by using one of the "discussion plays" as an example, especially "Heartbreak House," in which Shaw was under the congenial influence of Chekhovian dramaturgy and its movement by *non sequitur*. His later plays allow the same quality to become a major defect; in "The Millionairess," "Too True to Be Good," and "The Simpleton of the Unexpected Isles" event succeeds event with devil-may-care lack of logic, and remark follows remark with exaggerated Shavian caprice. Though the earlier plays manage to be convincing in spite of wild surface improbability, these later ones do not, and an important reason is that in them conversational continuity dips below the level of minimum plausibility.

There is no exact analogy in expository prose to the breaks between speeches in a play, and the most obvious place to look for lapses in sequence is at the intersections of sentences. Shaw's distinctive mode of transition is a subtle one, impossible to isolate and measure, but there are some methods he clearly does *not* favor. He does not, for one, begin many sentences with sequence indicators like "but," "therefore," "for," "and," and so on: in two chapters of the preface to "Saint Joan" (pp. 38–41) only four of twenty-six sentences begin this way. Nor does he use a particularly large number of pronouns to refer to previous sentences—eight in the whole twenty-six sentences ("it" five times, "such," "he" and "that" once each). This is really surprising considering how much of Shaw's writing is about people and things (see Chapter IV). He does not even carry words over from sentence to sentence as one might have expected of a writer whose allegiance is to similarity order.

The discourse develops along lines of contrast, movement

between general and particular, logical implications and so forth, just as any coherent discourse must; but the skeleton is delicate, hidden by flesh. In a typical sequence, sentence A states that "clerical direction posts"—official moral systems— coerce people when given a chance; sentence B, which begins "When the Church was a temporal as well as a spiritual power," exemplifies the proposition of A, but does so without any specific verbal sign of the relationship between them. C begins "Today, when the doctor has succeeded to the priest . . ." *Two* transitional relationships are evident here: one with A, as another example of its generalization, and one with B, as a contrast; yet no hint of an overt transition makes this clear. Sentence D is by way of explaining C; it opens with a general statement, "Our credulity is grosser than that of the Middle Ages," but no casual word ties it to C. E begins with "Also," but F is free-floating, and so is G, though they are bound to each other and to E in a relationship of contrast. And so forth. In this Shaw profits by comparison with more explicit authors, for the power of his thought is such that it fuses sentences together in logical and rhetorical patterns that are lucid without being belabored. Nevertheless, reliance on implicit connections rather than overt transition shows continuity taking a back seat stylistically. And the back seat becomes a rumble seat in some of Shaw's very late prose, where pontification, fact, personal anecdote, and invective succeed each other in the gayest disorder.[13]

This softening of transitions has as its corollary a tendency to epigram, for epigrams take their peculiar color not only from pithiness and generality, but from being syntactically abrupt. Admittedly they sometimes occur in the middle of a long sentence, or surrounded by "neverthelesses" and "on-the-other-hands," but much more typically they have a sentence or a clause to themselves. And in any case, they interrupt continuity because their compactness demands a different kind of interpretation from the usual. They must be peeled open, savored, digested, not merely sniffed. This effort Shaw asks of his reader with some regularity.

One last category of Shavian discontinuity should be mentioned: organization of the work as a whole. Since he claims to be relatively careless about plotting in his plays—he creates the *characters*, and then "lets them rip"—it is no surprise that his prefaces and essays lack rigorous planning. A symptom of this casualness is the habit he has of dividing long essays up into minute chapters ("Androcles" has eighty-four, *The Intelligent Woman's Guide*, eighty-six). No doubt this arrangement is partly designed as a convenience to the reader, but it is the consequence equally of Shaw's antipathy for sustained units of argument. Often the beginning of a new chapter is the beginning of a new tack as well, and in his two full-length books especially Shaw lets the argument carry him where it will. The evils of capitalism are all of a piece in his mind, without clear lines of precedence. This is as one would expect, for, to a writer whose conceptual system is organized around similarity, the category "evils of capitalism" might easily seem capacious enough to include almost every social phenomenon, and cohesive enough to render all sub-categories irrelevant.

In *Everybody's Political What's What?* many of the chapters make no pretense at all of following naturally from their predecessors, and others proceed by stream-of-consciousness logic. Thus he entitles three consecutive chapters "The Aesthetic Man," "The Man of Science," and "The Medical Man," but the titles themselves are enough to sate Shaw's appetite for parallelism: in the chapters he progresses casually from art and censorship to Pavlov and vivisection, to vaccination and socialized medicine. The next chapter is titled "Architecture a World Power," and begins, with triumphant irrelevance to medical ethics, "Architecture is a tremendous weapon in the aesthetic armory of the statesman." This excursion takes Shaw into sectarian architecture, which reminds him of religion and allows him to call the next chapter "The Theocratic Man"—back on the trail again. The impetus of this category ("men of different sorts"?) carries him through two more chapter titles, "The Collective Biologist" and "The Collective Statistician," which are a natural pair, but quite unrelated to the theocratic man. Shaw has as much trouble ending this book as Schubert had with some of his symphonies,[14] for how can there be a stopping place when there has been no original plan? Although while he was writing the book Shaw told Beatrice Webb that "the attempt to put my senile drivelings into some sort of intelligible order is very humiliating,"[15] his abstinence from organization is not to be blamed on senility, for in the page-to-page arguments Shaw is nearly as sharp as he had ever been. Rather it stems, I think, from an increasing abandonment to what was always his natural bent, from a kind of mental arthritis that leaves the joints in their old positions but stiffens them.

Under the heading of discontinuity I have, Shawlike, bundled together a miscellaneous parcel of stylistic traits: word-coining, cliché-juggling, transition-hopping, paradox, redefinition, epigram, flippancy. I have tried to show a connection between them and Shaw's ethic of change. The conclusion to which all of this evidence and the evidence of Chapter I strongly impels one is that his conceptual scheme grants more play to similarity than to contiguity—in fact, that he makes a virtue of rejecting the logic of contiguity. To disturb the sequence of the stylistic flow is for him as appealing a business as to whip up a tempest in the placid flow of moral tradition.

From the serio-comic congeries of impulses that combine in his personality, critics used to have difficulty extracting the "real" Shaw. Could he possibly be so funny, and yet serious? One crux where his humor and his moral passion meet, I believe, is the preference for discontinuity. Those things are funny, on the whole, which defy expectation, particularly events or situations that display reality at a disadvantage by contrast with the ideal order of things. Laughter is one way of dealing with the inadequacies of life, the solecisms of experience. By embracing the comic mode, therefore, Shaw gratifies doubly his appetite for discontinuity: he adopts a technique that works by incongruity, and he employs that technique in the service of social change. It is probably no coincidence that his particular brand of seriousness occurs in conjunction with his particlar brand of comedy, or that he claims membership in "the Church where the oftener you laugh the better, because by laughter only can you destroy evil without malice" (Theatres, I, viii).

3. OF ENTROPY AND REDUNDANCY

I propose to end my discussion of stylistic dicontinuity by stepping back to a new theoretical perspective.

To begin with, a critic who analyzes Shaw's style must take at least some notice of his contempt for the notion of style, of which the following statements give a hint:

a true original style is never achieved for its own sake. . . . Effectiveness of assertion is the Alpha and Omega of style. He who has nothing to assert has no style and can have none: he who has something to assert will go as far in power of style as its momentousness and his conviction will carry him. (M&S, xxxviii)

I have never aimed at style in my life: style is a sort of melody that comes into my sentences by itself: If a writer says what he has to say as accurately and effectively as he can, his style will take care of itself, if he has a style. (Imm, xliii)

Well, this is healthy medicine for the hereditary malady of Pater and his offspring, yet it is no more than a hundred other people have said, and it certainly does not mean that Shaw imitated Butler by writing off the cuff—on the contrary, he rewrote and polished assiduously. He claims, admittedly, that his care is all for content, that he may wrestle over what to say, but "the words come with the thought."[16] And although this may seem a quibble, Shaw is probably right in saying that he emphasized thought. The writer who has nothing fresh to say may have a style, but he will probably not have a very interesting one. All he can do in the nature of his case is assert things that are already familiar, and in prose with no novelty of content there can be only a spurious novelty of style. When thought runs in ruts, style cannot wreak violence on the reader's expectations. If Shaw had not rebelled against the morally and intellectually commonplace he would probably not have written such surprising prose.

Victor Erlich quotes the Russian Formalist Shklovskij as saying that to live is to grow accustomed both to the external world and to the words people commonly utter, so that "what has remained is mere recognition" in day-to-day ingestion of experience.[17] The writer counteracts this pull of habit by an "act of creative deformation," according to the Formalists. He makes the familiar strange, and thus rouses mind and feeling from their epistemic slumbers. This view of literature as irregularity, exactly opposite to the classical idea of generality, need not be swallowed whole, but the emphasis it places on oddity is suggestive. It draws an intimate connection between surprise and the power of literature to interpret life, to inform.

Another discipline that makes a rather similar point is communication theory.[18] Developed by telephone engineers, this science uses its key term, "information," in a strange but interesting way. It is not to be equated with "meaning," for meaning is a characteristic of individual words and messages, while information is a characteristic of the situation in which words or messages are being used. Suppose that one witness under oath is allowed only to say Yes or No to each question, while another responds as he likes. The second witness communicates more information both in the ordinary sense and in the technical sense of communication theorists: in the ordinary sense because he "says more," and in the technical sense because he has more *freedom of choice*. Information, to quote Warren Weaver, "relates not so much to what you *do* say as as to what you *could* say."[19] It is, obviously, a matter of statistical probability, and differs in this way from meaning, but the two have at least something in common.

A man using a language is faced with a series of choices; he must follow one signal with another. At each point of choice a certain amount of information is possible, and that amount depends partly on how many different signals are available, partly also on how nearly equal the various signals are in frequency of occurrence. Given a fixed number of signals, information at any point in a message is limited by the extent to which some are more likely than others. Now the likelihood of a certain signal may be low either because it is very rare throughout all messages of the language or because it is rare in conjunction with the signals that immediately precede it. Information can therefore be limited either by inequities in total frequency of the signals or by rigid sequential rules. The language as a whole loses in power to transmit information as statistical probabilities increase, and free choice correspondingly decreases. A language with high predictability is "redundant," in the sense that only a fraction of its maximum capacity is used, and the language with low predictability is characterized by high "entropy," or randomness (a *good* thing in information theory).

These definitions, created for work with codes, have at least some application to natural languages like English or to idiolects like Bernard Shaw's English. At the beginning of a sentence, "the" is quite likely to occur, both in that it is an extremely common word, and in that the syntactic position (following a pause) favors it. "Goes" is unlikely to occur because of sequential rules though it too is a common word. "Zymurgy" will not often occur because of its rarity in the language. In the context "as a matter of_____," the words "fact," "course," "form," "policy," and "principle" are all rather probable, for syntax permits them, they all occur often in this particular slot, and they are common in the language as a whole. Syntax rules against "is"; rarity in this context against "sun"; and rarity in the language against "zymogenesis." The information of both these contexts, then, is quite limited by a complicated system of probabilities. The same is true to a greater or lesser extent of every context in English, so that its redundancy as a "code" is clearly quite high.[20] As a linguist puts it, each word or phrase in a discourse partly determines the next—"raises the threshold" against most words and lowers it for a few.[21] Since high redundancy means low entropy and low information, it would seem to be a deficiency. Actually a certain amount of redundancy is a necessity, at least in the spoken language, because not every sound or every word is heard accurately,[22] and inequities in probability allow the listener a reasonable chance to fill in lacunae by using his vast though unconscious knowledge of syntactical rules and probabilities of all sorts.

But in the written language I do not see why redundancy need be nearly so high, unless to allow faster reading. And indeed, many of the best writers create idiolects of higher entropy by telescoping or dilating syntax, by using a wide range of vocabulary, and even by inventing words. That is one reason why Joyce, James, Faulkner, and the like are "hard" to read; in critical terms, they achieve greater *compactness* or *economy* of expression. The same process is much more common to verse, where the creative deformation that Erlich speaks of is most noticeable.

Shaw is no Joyce in these matters. But the stylistic evidence of this chapter does show him upsetting probabilities, building discontinuity, rejecting fixed sequences. As he weakens the force of "rules," he increases the uncertainty of any given word's following another, and thereby adds to the entropy of his "code."[23] The resulting increment of information is probably what leads critics to say that his style has a fast pace, for a style that exploits surprise avoids well-worn patterns that allow the reader to drowse, and makes him stay alert. Shaw himself prefers to express it by saying that his style is original because he has something to assert; by making his style carry a full load of "information," he keeps it an efficient worker. And, what is perhaps more important, he keeps it interesting. This is not the highest flattery that can be given a writer, but it is well up among words of praise. A good reply to the accusation that Shaw is merely a self-conscious *enfant terrible* is to say that the techniques of shock are techniques by which language is kept fresh and thought is kept alive.

III

The Posture of Opposition

It is an instinct with me personally to attack every idea
which has been full grown ten years.
—"Our Theatres in the Nineties"

T<small>HE</small> epigraph points to a partial repetition here of some material from the last chapter. I shall also be doing a reprise with variations of some themes from Chapter I. The excuse for such a rear-guard action is partly the obvious one that only an analysis of the greatest artificiality can rigidly compartmentalize the stylistic traits of a writer whose habits of expression form a complex and integrated pattern. But the main reason for going back and having another look is that the angle of vision will be somewhat different this time. My subject to this point has been connections between Shaw's basic epistemic mode and its stylistic repercussions. From here on I shall be concerned less with style as a way of knowing and increasingly with the rhetorical and emotional uses to which that way of knowing is put. To take a specific example, I have contended that the Shavian series testifies to a habit of "leveling." The question remains whether Shaw uses such catalogues in order to attack or support, to exult or complain, to explicate or insist. A writer makes language bend to his characteristic way of experiencing things, but he shapes it also to express favorite postures, attitudes, and rhetorical roles. To the study of such things I shall give more attention in this chapter and the next.

1. BORN TO SET IT RIGHT

In making himself the critic of things as they are, Shaw places himself in the position of outsider. Everyone, to be sure, can imagine a better world than the present one; everyone has some grievances. But Shaw does not want the *status quo* merely doctored up a bit, and few can face such a wholesale scrapping of traditions as he does propose. The poor, who might profit by revolution, have no voice, and even if they had they would balk at many of Shaw's iconoclasms—his attacks on marriage and conventional religion, for example. The middle class, the very group that leans most heavily on established institutions, is the class with a voice to use in defending them. Thus Shaw finds that "civilized society is one huge bourgeoisie" (M&S, xv), and that to be against the middle class is to be against almost everybody. Enemy of the people (for their own good) is therefore a role that meshes naturally with Shaw's ideas. It is also intensely congenial to him just as a stance.

Shaw was born into a family that asked (and deserved) little tribute of reverence. He did look up to his father at first, until he discovered that the senior Shaw, who liked to give thunderous lectures on the evils of drink, was himself a tippler. This revelation of hypocrisy and weakness left a scar on Shaw's attitude toward parental authority. His mother, long-suffering and admirably talented, was nonetheless too remote and cold a figure to be idealized. He was surrounded, too, by various eccentric uncles—one whose "profanity and obscenity in conversation were of Rabelaisian exuberance" (SSS, 15), and one who went harmlessly insane—and watched over by a kind of surrogate father, the musician Lee, who ate unfashionable brown bread and criticized doctors, and whose influence on Shaw's home "accustomed me to the scepticism as to academic authority which still persists in me" (SSS, 14). Hardly a conventional group of sacrosanct elders.

But more important still was the atmosphere of laxity that surrounded the young George Bernard. The children were treated as adults, left to their own devices unencumbered by demands for obedience, by guidance, or by love; their upbringing lacked both Victorian austerity and Victorian sentimentality. No one attempted to nurture in Shaw a sense of sin. Quite the contrary, in fact. His father would occasionally rebuke him for scoffing at the Bible, but would conclude the defense by stating, "with an air of perfect fairness, that even the worst enemy of religion could say no worse of the Bible than that it was the damndest parcel of lies ever written" (Imm, xxiii). Deaths were common in Shaw's big family, and to save time at funerals the family coaches would maintain a lugubrious pace only until reaching the city limits, then tear at a gallop to the burial ground, which lay some distance away, while the family often passed the time by speaking ill of the deceased. Mockery of death and mockery of religion were appropriately set against a background of Mrs. Shaw's music, and punctuated by Mr. Shaw's drunken sprees. And yet at the same time the family maintained the most absurd pretensions of superiority: they were after all Protestants; they were descended from gentry, albeit unimpressively; they were in wholesale, not retail, trade, and Shaw's father could criticize him for playing with the son of an ironmonger. Of this class snobbery Shaw remarks, "I remember Stopford Brooke one day telling me that he discerned in my books an intense and contemptuous hatred for society. No wonder!"[1] Sensitive to this hypocrisy, and receptive to the permissiveness and skepticism, Shaw seems never to have felt awe toward authority, seems almost to have been "born free from many of the venerations and inhibitions which restrain the tongues of most small boys," as he said to Hesketh Pearson.[2] In any case he is always ready to ridicule his elders, from his own father to cultural father-figures like Darwin.

If his family origins disinclined him to accept the world as he found it, education stamped his skepticism in still more deeply. His schooling "operated by a succession of eye-openers each involving the repudiation of some previously held belief, and consequently of my conviction of my father's infallibility," so that he thinks the learning process a "ceremony of disillusion" (EPWW, 155) at each step of advance. Nor did his informal education—Marx, Henry George, Bellamy—do anything to dilute his conviction that whatever is is misunderstood, and that most of what is is wrong. His first novel, *Immaturity*, ends symbolically with a negative shake of the hero's head.

Throughout his life Shaw wrote as an *opponent;* and this stance had its origins in his reaction against the entrenched Victorian smugness which prevailed during his boyhood and through his first quarter-century in London. It has become fashionable lately to deny that the Victorians were smug, and to see them instead as deeply troubled by the crumbling of old creeds and the mushrooming of new problems. This is true, certainly, of the great writers, but their voices gain in heroic timbre precisely because of the emptiness into which they cry.

In the face of their jeremiads the great bourgeoisie remains complacent and conservative, as perhaps it always has been. It is against that conservatism—against a collective mind that is shocked by the New Woman, thinks socialists cads, subscribes to a comfortably tailored blend of middle-class Christianity and scientific materialism, and holds all kinds of selfish cant as gospel—that Shaw writes.

During the Spanish-American War he read an account of an American commander who, upon seeing the Spanish fleet burned, gathered his men together and declared his belief in God Almighty. On reading this, Shaw concluded that "if I am sane, the rest of the world ought not to be at large. We cannot both see things as they really are."[3] Not infrequently his critiques of society do give the impression that Shaw is the only sane man in a world of the feebleminded and the deluded, but at least this egotism stems more from a conviction of the world's folly than from a sense of his own infallibility. Though he sometimes says, "How right I am!" he more often says, "How misguided the others are!" And against their madness he sets himself to write.

At the end of his life he describes the Shavian crusade against error:

My Everybody's What's What is only an attempt by a very ignorant old man to communicate to people still more ignorant than himself such elementary social statics as he has managed to pick up . . . in the course of a life . . . spent largely in discovering and correcting the mistakes into which his social antecedents and surroundings led him. (EPWW, 366)

The cardinal truth about society is that it lacks knowledge and self-awareness: "What is wrong with the prosaic Englishman

is what is wrong with the prosaic men of all countries: stupidity"
(M&S, xix). For their stupidity his home remedy is a heavy dose
of truth, administered by himself, but he sees their ignorance
as so deep and so soothing that they desperately resist enlightenment. Thus he has it that audiences and critics rejected "Too
True to Be Good" because its honesty had been too much for
them, "as if I had hit them in some new and unbearably sore
spot" (Too True, 3).

Throughout *What I Really Wrote About the War* he adopts
the role of Cassandra, or the voice in the wilderness: in wartime
people hunger for palliation with special acuteness. To Shaw,
"Common Sense About the War," in spite of its relative sanity,
seems "the cruelest use I have ever had to make of my pen."
He would like to have spared amiable people the "unbearable"
truth about power diplomacy, but "could not indulge these
innocents" because his business "was to clear our case of false
claims" (War, 116–17). Elsewhere he speaks of "Common
Sense" as "that intolerable document which afterwards turned
out to be so exasperatingly right in every detail" (p. 388), and
of the people's "prayers to be shielded from that terrible thing,
the truth" (p. 48). One article ends: "I can promise nothing
beyond another unheeded cry in the wilderness" (p. 394); and
another begins: "I told you so" (p. 395). At the same period
he was writing the Webbs that after thirty years of telling
Englishmen "the truth as far as human judgment is capable of
the truth, I find that they remain invincibly persuaded that I
am a mischief maker, a liar, and a wrecker."[4] In all this he is
unquestionably sincere, yet he brings extra gusto to the part
because it so admirably suits his self-image of Shaw the facer of
unpopular truths and shatterer of illusions, Shaw the opposer,

Shaw the wise fool. Unsurprisingly, it is a part that he assigns to some of the most memorable figures in his work: Owen Jack and Sidney Trefusis in the novels, Captain Shotover, Jack Tanner, Saint Joan, and many others in the plays.

Shaw's choice of allies throws into relief his choice of role. Against Victorian well-being he champions the cosmic uneasiness of Schopenhauer, Nietzsche, Butler, Marx, Ruskin, Morris, and Carlyle, and the artistic rebelliousness of Wagner, Ibsen, Chekhov, Gorky, and the French Impressionists. For reinforcement he throws Jesus at the establishment. In this company alone Shaw feels at ease.

With this posture of revolt, his preference for change (as outlined in Chapter II) jibes nicely. A civilization cannot progress, cannot remake itself, except through the destruction of old institutions: "Every step of progress means a duty repudiated, and a scripture torn up" (QI, 20). To change is to deny the claims of what is. To conventional people, therefore, progress seems regress, for it always entails the relinquishing of previous advances and once-revolutionary ideals. Such people denounce as an enemy of society the free spirit who mocks ideals, though he is actually performing a service by "sweeping the world clear of lies" (QI, 45). Shaw does accept the necessity of social rules—thus his rejection of anarchism for its "terrifying danger and obvious inconvenience" (QI, 320)—but no law is so absolute that it can stand up forever, and all laws, creeds, and systems of ethics, "instead of making society better than its best unit, make it worse than its average unit, because they are never up to date" (QI, 317). Thus the duty of the man of genius with a conscience is almost invariably to attack, since many can be found to defend. The worst philistines of all are journalists and artists who take it as their duty merely to *reflect* the "ignorance and prejudice of their readers" (QI, 330), rather than trying to reform them.

It is worth noting, apropos of Shaw's contrariness, that he does not rest content with assaults on the enemy's weak points. Rightly he contrasts himself with Molière, who makes his doctors mercenary humbugs, and with Dickens, who attacks revivalist preachers by having Stiggins first get drunk on pineapple rum and finally be kicked into a horse trough. Shaw "strikes at Hector or Achilles, not at Thersites."[5] It has often been remarked that most of his dramatic villains make a strong case for themselves. Such devil's disciples as Mrs. Warren, Morell, the Inquisitor, and the Devil himself in "Man and Superman" are far from being straw men or buffoons. Similarly, he directs his satire and invective at such able opponents as the medical profession, experimental science, Darwinism, conventional theism, and the free enterprise system. He generally strikes at the pillars of society, not at the aberrations.

As I have pointed out, Shaw considers wholesale rebellion such as this essential to progress, and his argument for tolerance turns on the necessity for granting as much leeway as society can bear to the discontented servants of the Life Force. Yet on the subject of tolerance Shaw has conflicting feelings. There is much of the authoritarian in his intellectual make-up: his intolerance of mediocrity, his passion for social order, his hatred for random drifting, all put him out of patience with the painfully lethargic movements of a free society. Some of this impatience spills over into tempered admiration of Mussolini, Stalin, even Hitler, and into such rigid systems as state-controlled genetics. But the pressure of his relentless individualism is too powerful for this other complex of motives. A fully disciplined society might take it upon itself to hamstring its Wagners, Ibsens, and Shaws, and the moral claustrophobia in England is quite severe enough without contemplating such anti-utopian extensions of authority. So Shaw consistently supports freedom. He reluctantly accepts democracy as the means of transition to communism; compulsion will not work because "we *hate* masters" (Essays, 89). He stoutly opposes censorship because "an attack on morals may turn out to be the salvation of the race" (Dilemma, 385). And he writes tracts proposing a bill of rights for children and "controversial education" to "tear away the camouflage from commercial civilization" (Delusions, 332). The act of opposition is as necessary to the human race as the sexual act, and must be jealously protected from the anxious reprisals of the ins. Shaw has ambiguous feelings about authority, but finally he is neither contradictory nor vague in his advocacy of tolerance.

In her study of perception in prejudiced and unprejudiced children Else Frenkel-Brunswik finds a correlation too great to be fortuitous between intolerance of perceptual and conceptual ambiguity and "strength of hostility, of power-orientation, of externalization, and of rigid stereotyping."[6] This conjunction has more than passing interest; I suggested in Chapter I that Shaw is inhospitable toward conceptual ambiguity, and in this chapter that his characteristic authorial stance is in part hostile. There is no need to seek a too rigorous application of Frenkel-Brunswik's terms. Shaw is power-oriented only in being immensely *interested* in power, not in wanting to prostrate himself before it. He stereotypes his opponents only to the extent of finding them all lacking in wit. As for "externalization" of ag-

gressions and weaknesses, that is the mark of a paranoid, and
to call Shaw a paranoid would be to substitute diagnosis for
literary criticism. Shaw has good reason for thinking himself
besieged by enemies, since he goes so far out of his way to
create them.[7] "Hostility," finally, has some connotations quite
inappropriate to Shaw's outlook on life; he is too warm-blooded
and too flamboyant to decapitate his enemies with any emotion
but the warrior's joy of battle. But if Frenkel-Brunswik's terms
do not pin Shaw down like a botanical specimen, they do at
least come close. Hand in hand with Shaw the man of genius
goes Shaw the antagonist, the gadfly, the outrager of stodgy
people, the opponent of majorities. I have laid some of his lapses
in common sense (antivivisection, etc.) at the door of rigid
categorizing; they also reflect, obviously, his unwillingness to
be on the side of the majority or to find repose in yea-saying.
In the light of such alternate explanations it is especially convenient to find psychologists linking the epistemic stance of the
leveler with the rhetorical stance of the nay-sayer.

2. n o, N o, N O

The passage that follows is an example of Shaw playing the
patient man of reason, beleaguered by the intolerable pig-
headedness of the vivisectors. Anyone who knows the ABC of
Science, he says, knows that men must not seek knowledge by
criminal methods:

He knows that there are fifty ways of ascertaining any fact; that only
the two or three worst of them are dirty ways; that those who deliberately choose the dirty ways are not only morally but intellectually imbecile; that the "clean-handed man with the scalpel" is a
humbug who has to buy his brains from the instrument maker; that
it is ridiculous to expect that an experimenter who commits acts of

[handwritten] cannot *[?]* 1·5·0·2·2

[handwritten signature] G.B. Shaw Esq.

To "THE BOOKMAN'S JOURNAL", 19, Buckingham Street, Strand, W. C. 2.

(1) Have we your name
and address correct?... *I don't know*
(Please repeat here
(as a check........ *Bernard Shaw   10 Adelphi Terrace   London W.C.2*

(2) Are you interested in
(a) BOOKS......... *No. No.*
or (b) PRINTS............ *No. No.*
or (c) both?................ *No.*

(3) Do you collect
either of the above?... *No*

(4) Do you invite the
general catalogues of
(a) Secondhand booksellers......
(b) Printsellers................   *NO*
(c) New Booksellers?.,.............

(5) In what special subjects
are you interested? :-
(a) BOOKS..........   *NO*
(b) PRINTS.................

(6) Do you wish for
special catalogues or
reports of 5a or 5b............   *NO*   *NO*

(7) Is there any other
information you care to give?..............

add other
names and
addresses
(8) The names and addresses   overleaf if
of any book-collectors   required.
you know who should be
in this record?.....................................   *NO*

(9) Do you wish to order a
copy of the Record when
published? (If so a prospectus will be sent in due course)..   *NO*

Note: Kindly insert "yes" or "no" (or the information asked for) in
each case for the sake of clarity.

This form is not for booksellers.

diabolical cruelty for the sake of what he calls Science can be trusted
to tell the truth about the results; that no vivisector ever accepts
another vivisector's conclusions nor refrains from undertaking a fresh
set of vivisections to upset them; that as any fool can vivisect and
gain kudos by writing a paper describing what happened, the lab-
oratories are infested with kudos hunters who have nothing to tell
that they could not have ascertained by asking a policeman except
when it is something that they should not know (like the sensations
of a murderer); and that as these vivisectors crowd humane research
workers out of the schools and discredit them, they use up all the
endowments and bequests available for their purposes, leaving nothing for serious physiological research. (Delusions, 142–43)

Anybody may know this, but Shaw tells him all the same. Each
of his "that" clauses denies one proposition in the vivisectionists'
creed, and the sentence amounts to a demolition job on the
whole structure of their argument. Often when Shaw gets up
steam for one of the these colossal series, his fires are those of
anger. The syntactical heaping-up that betokens a similarity
relationship also serves him rhetorically, to smother his audience, as it were: he confronts the opposition, not with one argument, but with ten. Such superabundance has special propriety
in the crusade against entrenched opinion, which needs to be
jostled rudely before it can be dislodged. Note, too, the language
of exaggeration in this passage—"fifty ways of ascertaining any
fact," "it is ridiculous," "diabolical cruelty," "no vivisector ever,"
"any fool," "have nothing to tell," "all the endowments," "leaving
nothing." Hyperbole, like the Shavian catalogue, can be understood in terms both of the epistemology of equivalence and of
the rhetoric of opposition.

The same holds true for the devices of comparison. One
of Shaw's favorites contains an explicit form of negation, "no

more___than___." But he uses the others to deny or contradict almost as regularly. His analogies seek measuring sticks for the villainy or illogicality of his opponents, and his comparisons of degree often work by *reductio ad absurdum* ("could not manage a baked potato stand honestly and capably, much less a coal mine"—IWG, 122). When he highlights the similarities between one period and another he often does so pejoratively in order to emphasize the moral corruption of both; here, for example, he presses both the series and the "as" of equality into such a comparison:

Already in the twentieth century there has been as much brute coercion and savage intolerance, as much flogging and hanging, as much impudent injustice on the bench and lustful rancor in the pulpit, as much naive resort to torture, persecution, and suppression of free speech and freedom of the press, as much war, as much of the vilest excess of mutilation, rapine, and delirious indiscriminate slaughter of helpless non-combatants, old and young . . . as we can find any record of from the days when the advocacy of liberty was a capital offence and Democracy was hardly thinkable. (Mis, 103–4)

The catalogue bulges with invective and exaggeration, as Shaw annihilates the ascription of tolerance and humanity to his contemporaries. One could follow the thread of opposition through other equivalence forms, and through the forms of discontinuity as well—particularly semantic shock, redefinition, word-coining, and paradox. But it will be more profitable at this point to scan new and more concentrated evidence of denial and opposition.

To begin with macrostylistics, Shaw frequently compounds the structure of a whole piece from a set of negations. Take that quintessence of Shavianism, "The Revolutionist's Handbook."

After a preface concluding that "Revolutions have *never* light-
ened the burden of tyranny" (italics mine), John Tanner's first
chapter outlines the need for controlled breeding, but in doing
so it begins with a denial that transfiguration of institutions is
ever more than change from Tweedledum to Tweedledee, and
ends with a warning that the goal of breeding must be neither
a race of mindless athletes nor a race of Sunday School prigs.
Chapter Two also carries a burden of negation: it brushes aside
the twin obstacles of property and marriage; rejecting first the
revolutionist's contention that they are important; second, the
idea that society will much feel their departure; and third,
the conventional notion that cohabitation and procreation are
necessarily connected. Then, via a discussion of the Oneida
community, Tanner disposes of the hope that great leaders and
great creeds can raise a people above its natural level. The
fourth chapter makes short work of the supposed objections of
human instinct to regimented genetics. With the fifth we are
back to the need for a race of supermen, the argument being
that democracy cannot thrive when the electorate has feet of
clay. Then another quick vault, this time to a denial that prudery
represents instinctive resistance to the Life Force. Chapter
Seven returns to political realities, and disposes of the ideas
(1) that social reform is a solution, (2) that violence is any help,
(3) that man has progressed during recorded history, and (4)
that he is even capable of progress without a mutation in character. The next chapter takes up the third of these denials, and
debunks a whole series of alleged modern achievements. With
Chapter Nine, Tanner returns to the denial that social progress
can occur, barring evolutionary progress. He concludes by rejecting the idea that breeding can be controlled in a *laissez-faire*

society—a devious way to arrive at the necessity of socialism!

On this gathering of positions Shaw imposes very little logical coherence; transitions are, as usual, his weak point. What does hold his arguments together is the posture of denial, for the little book stands united with itself against both the conventional dogmas of capitalism and those of socialism as well. Many of Shaw's arguments could as easily have been cast as affirmations rather than denials, but whenever possible he elects the negative mode, as if his positions will gain sharpness from being honed against those of imagined antagonists.[8]

The patterns of negation that give structure to Shaw's arguments are naturally reticulate in miniature on the level of sentence and phrase: one cannot constantly refute without ever saying "not," and negative forms abound in his prose. A single page from an open letter to Frank Harris contains thirteen of them:

you can learn nothing about your biographees from their sex histories
The sex relation is not a personal relation
could not endure one another for a day
you would be none the wiser
I was not impotent
I was not sterile
I was not homosexual
not promiscuously
I never associated
nor had any scruples
I was not attracted
my first adventure did not occur until
Do not misunderstand this   (SSS, 113)

Admittedly, Shaw is up on his hind legs here, and to a certain extent he is contradicting actual statements made by the improbable Harris. But the high incidence of negatives obtains elsewhere, though less spectacularly. To take a longer and more typical sample, six pages of *The Intelligent Woman's Guide* (pp. 360–65) contain, respectively, seven, nine, nine, eight, six, and twelve of these forms (thirty-five "nots," six "nos," five "nors," three "nevers," and two "nothings"), an incidence considerably higher than the norm for other writers.[9]

But such a rigidly limited measure of negation is far from telling the whole story. These same six pages, for instance, display a number of other forms of denial and opposition: "the *wrong* way to put it," "the very *last thing* the . . . worker wants," "the common trick of . . . is a foolish one," and so forth. To get at the full sweep of negation in Shaw's prose it is necessary to make a fuller and less formal analysis. Consider another page, this time from the Preface to "John Bull's Other Island" (JBOI, xvi). To begin with there are nine negative forms. In addition, there are several words that imply opposition or denial somewhat less directly: "without," "only" (implying a completeness not attained), and the prefixes "un-" and "out-" ("outwit," etc.). Then there are the signs of syntactical opposition, "although" and "instead." But the largest group of negative words are those that have a looser association with invective, those with negative connotations. In such words and phrases the passage abounds:

violently shoved	conspire	blockhead
stumbling blindly	assassinate	blockheads
backward	deeper and deeper	compelled
crush	shame	supercilious
weaknesses	lack	tongue-tied
terrors	enemy	exposing

misery	shams	denouncing
bayonets	hypocrisies	lose
embarrass	servitude	discount
bully	illusions	miss

Such words sustain the rhetoric of opposition not because of any formal characteristics but because of their meanings, and because of the freight of emotion associated with them, emotion whose burden is condemnatory. The total number of words I have enumerated so far is forty-eight, on a page that contains only some three-hundred-odd words all told: more than one word out of seven signals opposition.

This is about as far as measurement can go, but it still is not the limit of the passage's negativism. For one thing, syntactical juxtaposition sometimes works to bring out a conflict. For example, a sentence with an explicit negative—"We [Ireland] cannot crush England as a Pickford's van might crush a perambulator"—precedes one with no negative forms: "We are the perambulator and England the Pickford." The force of the earlier negative carries over into this sentence, so that its effect is to *deny* the suggestion that Ireland is stronger than England. In addition, the second sentence contains an internal opposition, the contrast between a Pickford and a perambulator, which is indicated only by the grammatical pairing of two words with disparate referents. As syntax works to diffuse an atmosphere of opposition, so does the tone of the whole section. "England" becomes a term of invective in itself, since in the context of Shaw's anti-imperialist argument England is the main villain. And in a series such as this: "a supercilious, unpopular, tongue-tied, aristocratic Protestant Parnell," the distaste attaching to the first three terms carries over to give "aristocratic" and

"Protestant" unfavorable connotations that they would not necessarily possess otherwise, and establishes "Parnell" as something to be against. To the effects of syntax and connotation must be added, finally, the effects of irony, which often serves to invert what would ordinarily be terms of approbation. Thus when Shaw speaks of "any mysterious Irish pluck, Irish honesty, Irish bias on the part of Providence, or sterling Irish solidity of character," he is deploring, not pluck and honesty themselves, but the Celtic sentimentality that insists on taking such virtues as the special property of the Irish. Irony, as a means of speaking to the happy few over the heads of the ignorant many, is necessarily a weapon of critical attack.

I do not suggest that every page of Shaw's prose has its feet so firmly planted in a pugilistic stance, but only that he finds this stance especially congenial. The page I have been analyzing does not strike me as an unparalleled example of Shavian invective, but as one fairly easy to match in his work. His chosen role as the unwelcome sage and his image of the public as desperately clinging to soothing lies make it inevitable that he should spend much of his energy flaying complacency and disputing received opinion.

3. PROSE AGAINST ITSELF

Unity, says Shaw, is fatal to the drama, which must present a conflict. But, he goes on, "the obvious conflicts of unmistakeable good with unmistakeable evil can only supply the crude drama of villain and hero. . . . In such cheap wares I do not deal" (PPU, II, ix). Certainly this self-appraisal is on the whole just. Although many of the plays have one or two hopeless snobs or ignoramuses, out-and-out villains do not abound. Normally, if there *is* a devil, he is so eloquently his own advocate that Shaw himself seems half convinced. To think of the complexity of debate in the better plays is to be reminded of the complexity of judgment they require—the awareness, for instance, that both Joan and her judges have a measure of right on their side, or that Andrew Undershaft is only Prince of Darkness in the sense of having made himself prince in a place where darkness is the natural condition. Shaw habitually forestalls the stock response, says No to the reader's facile verdicts. The dazzling brightness of Shavian dialogue would be impossible if half the burden fell to straw men.

In another context he claims that this dramatic many-sidedness extends to all of his thinking: "My inborn dramatic faculty and professional habit as a playwright prevent me from taking a one-sided view . . ." (War, 23). Now this is a contention that needs to be received with more caution than the other one. Shaw is certainly not one-sided in the sense of being narrow, and he is emphatically not one-sided in the sense of cleaving blindly to an already-formed position in a controversy. But it is nonetheless impossible to see in his prose the cautious, prudent thinker, weighing all possibilities and coming judiciously to rest on one of them with only tentative force. The typical Shavian idea may be idiosyncratic and complex, but once he has adopted it he pushes it on the reader with a quite one-sided tenacity.

The common ground between his dramatic dialogue and his discursive prose is not urbane broadmindedness, but scrappiness. His prose, like his drama, bulges with conflicting voices, full of argument. Since, in the drama, there can hardly be an authorial voice with final jurisdiction over the disputants, the devil always seems to getting his due. But in the prose his arguments collapse under an avalanche of Shavian scorn; Shaw articulates them in order to drown them out with his own commanding rhetoric. Still, the rejected arguments play an important stylistic part. As the forces of the enemy they elicit the negatives that I have already discussed; but negation is impossible without something to be denied, and it still remains for me to examine the actual stylistics of tension and conflict.

In Chapter II, I argued that directional shifts from speech to speech in the plays have a loose parallel in various forms of syntactical discontinuity that appear in the prose. It is possible to find an even closer analogy for these dramatic shifts in the give and take, mostly give on Shaw's part, between his persona and the opposition. Consider the short sentence of denial, which dismisses arguments that have gone immediately before, thus reversing the direction of the discourse. Such sentences range from the relatively formal and moderate—

So that will not do. (IWG, 6–7)
They did not strike me in that way. (HH, 3)
This was a bad beginning. (Dilemma, 370)

to the relatively curt and disrespectful—

They are not. (IWG, 1)
This is impossible. (IWG, 2)
They won't. (IWG, 44)
Stuff and nonsense. (IWG, 7)
That is stupid. (Delusions, 198)
No. (Too True, 16)

These rejoinders signal conflict rather spectacularly, because of the brevity and abruptness with which they reverse the direction of the argument, and they are a favorite trick of Shaw's. But of course even for him they represent a tiny fraction of all the oscillation between assertion and denial. The transitional words that mark concession and conflict—words such as "although," "but," and "yet"—are responsible for very many changes of direction. Shaw probably does not rely more heavily on these commonplace rhetorical shifts than the average writer, since large units of his prose move in unbroken lines like those of the torrential series (see Chapter I). But a count of such changes of direction as constitute a *denial* of what went before, rather than a mere *qualification*, reveals the extent to which Shaw's prose moves by negation.[10] An unusually large number of the junctions between sentence and sentence involve a collision of opposed forces.

This simple method of giving the opposition its brief say while denying its claims with some kind of negative has an analogue in these slightly less compact forms:

It is not true that all the atrocities of Capitalism are the expression of human vice and evil will: on the contrary . . . (EPWW, 2)

It is not that science is free from legends, witchcraft, miracles, biographic boostings of quacks as heroes and saints, and of barren scoundrels as explorers and discoverers. On the contrary . . . (Back, lxxix–lxxx)

Here Shaw allots a sentence or clause to the view he is rejecting, but two things are worth noting: First, although he does not state his refutation until after he has presented the opposite contention, he nullifies that contention before it can gain a toehold by subordinating it grammatically to a main clause that *denies* it—"It is not true that . . ." Second, the position Shaw

refutes is put so uncompromisingly that it would claim no credence even if preserved from Shaw's contradiction. He makes no
pretense of giving a fair hearing to the accused, whose testi-
mony he exaggerates in order to point up the dichotomy of
right and wrong views. The conflict created by such oppositions
is the resolved tension of a mind already made up, rather than
the balanced tension of indecision and careful weighing.

The same holds true of several shorter forms in the "not
_____, but_____" family:

Not against the opinions it expresses, but against the facts it records.
(QI, 175)

Socialism is not charity nor loving-kindness, nor sympathy with the
poor, nor popular philanthropy . . . but the economist's hatred of
waste and disorder, the aesthete's hatred of ugliness and dirt, the
lawyer's hatred of injustice . . . (EPWW, 78)

picture postcards might have been sold of her as a general: they
would not have been sold of her as a sultana. (StJ, 9)

neither sown nor reaped, baked nor brewed, but only collected from
the hungry . . . (IWG, 348)

This pattern of denial and affirmation is a rather common one
in Shaw's prose. It leads to a species of semantic overlap, since
to tell what is not the case in the same breath that one tells what
is the case is to specify a situation doubly. But the semantic
redundancy is not a rhetorical redundancy. In buttressing his
assertion with a negation he exposes to scorn either the folly of
the other side's views or the venality of its actions. It is important to Shaw not only that truth be broadcast, but that error be
pilloried, and the "not_____, but_____" pattern answers to both
aims.

When the opposition has its say within such a short syntactical span, the entire process of refutation can easily be tucked into the pocket of a larger grammatical garment. Take, for example, the by-now-familiar Shavian series, itself an instrument of denial as a whole. Within these catalogues the individual members may embody lesser conflicts. Thus when Shaw disputes the ability of censors to do their job he complains that they cannot distinguish "between art and blackguardism, between morality and virtue, between immorality and vice, between conscientious heresy and mere baseness of mind and foulness of mouth" (Dilemma, 410). Each phrase sets two things against each other that are, to Shaw, quite contradictory. On the four separate conflicts of ideas, the larger conflict between him and the censors depends. Here is a more gross example of tension within the units of a series: the government must assume, he says,

that everybody is exactly like everybody else, although no two people are alike; that everybody is consistent although everybody is in fact a sackful of contradictions; that all marriages are alike, all love affairs alike, all . . .; although they are all as different as fingerprints. (EPWW, 334)

In each of the three large sections of the series a position gets voiced and then rejected, with the effect of direct contradiction.

The trope of which both these series present special cases is, of course, antithesis, an important framework for stylistic opposition. In it, conflict emerges most dramatically when, as with the second of the two series, Shaw repeats a number of words, allowing their exact correspondence to emphasize the divergence of the others. Thus, in order to suggest the difference between democracy and justice, and dispel the notion that justice is a practical alternative to democracy, Shaw opposes them thus: "The indispensable preliminary to Democracy is the representation of every interest: the indispensable preliminary to justice is the elimination of every interest" (JBOI, xxvii–xxviii). In this respect democracy differs from justice as much as elimination does from representation. Neat opposites of this sort have a peculiar appeal for him:

Now the tendency of private property is to keep the masses mere beasts of burden. The tendency of Social Democracy is to educate them—to make men of them. (Essays, 59)

a mystic nexus to replace the cash nexus. (JBOI, 218)

When the Germans bombed the Cathedral of Rheims, the world rang with the horror of the sacrilege. When they bombed the Little Theatre . . . the fact was not even mentioned in the papers. (HH, 36)

They satisfy both the requirements of equivalence and those of conflict, for they compare two events or situations that are precisely alike in some ways and radically different in others.

When Shaw's antitheses build less on repetition of major words, they may build more on the pairing up of grammatical frames. For instance, "The economic change is merely formal: the moral change is enormous" (Essays, 12); or "On decent human terms with one another instead of on competitive capitalistic terms" (IWG, 154). The syntax of one half mirrors that of the other closely enough to show that the two *meanings* are far from alike. But such close repetition either of syntactical frames or of words themselves is more characteristic of neoclassical than of Shavian antithesis, which spreads out into a variety of forms. Its mechanism may be tripped by the repetition of just one word and the metamorphosis of one or two others:

"The business of an honest and understanding Government is . . . When Governments are either dishonest or ignorant . . ." (IWG, 292). There is no parallelism at all, nor any word pointing to negation, but the echo of "honest" in "dishonest" and the fainter echo of "understanding" in "ignorant" suffice to put the two sentences in evident conflict. Or the antithesis may emerge only through the total meanings of its parts, as when "soldiers who had done voluntary and heroic service in the field" are set against "persons who had apparently never run a risk or spent a farthing that they could avoid." (HH, 26).

This last is the most common, though not the most noticeable, method of Shavian antithesis. It matches nicely his conviction that society's make-up is badly askew, and his hope that merely exposing contradictions to the light will suffice to turn some readers against them. *The Intelligent Woman's Guide* is particularly full of such contrasts—one woman has a single pair of leaking boots and another has forty pairs of high-heeled shoes (p. 56); a nation is confused if it "spends money on champagne before it has provided milk for its babies" (p. 56); and so on. These contradictions are the nourishment on which socialism thrives, and as such they inevitably play a significant part in Shaw's political writing, but he favors such modes of contrast whether or not his subject is the sickness of capitalism. They are tightly implicated with typically Shavian debate.

When antithesis works merely by the juxtaposition of disparate meanings it may closely resemble paradox, which also deals in the oddities of reality. All that is needed to push many Shavian antitheses over the line into paradox is closer structuring to insist on the compatibility of seemingly incompatible meanings. Thus, when he says that "our laws make law impossible" (JBOI, 243), he relies on an antithesis between true law and false law to make sense of the apparent contradiction. As Bentley explains, Shaw often uses words in two different senses, "postulates a genuine article—gentleman, science, democracy—and in each case the spurious product which has stolen the market."[11] The paradox of "law" and "laws" is followed by another, "Our liberties destroy all freedom," which, instead of making the same word mean opposite things, makes two supposed synonyms work against each other as opposites. The list of capitalistic injustices moves on to property: "Our property is organized robbery"—another variety of paradox, which operates by equating two words normally taken to be antonyms. Similarly, "Our morality is an impudent hypocrisy." Then the form shifts again with "our wisdom is administered by inexperienced or malexperienced dupes, our power wielded by cowards and weaklings." Here the paradox turns on incongruity rather than overt contradiction. It is not impossible that power should be wielded by weaklings, but such a thing does violate one's sense of rightness. This catalogue of the hypocrisies entailed by a *laissez-faire* system concludes with still another form of paradox—oxymoron: "Our honor false in all its points." In this most compact of antitheses, the adjective undermines the noun. The variegation of this series suggests how numerous are the syntactical means by which Shaw sets up paradox. He falls into it naturally, without rhetorical or stylistic affectation, because it conforms to his vision of the contradictions in human conduct.

I have now run through the most obvious stylistic outcroppings of tension and conflict. A number of more subtle manifestations remain, but subtlety in these matters is really not Shaw's forte. It is possible, for instance, to imply an opposition by stating only one half of it. Thus, in describing medieval economic life, Shaw says, "If they catch a man buying goods solely in order to sell them a few hours later at a higher price, they treat that man as a rascal," and the man never pleads that it is his "pious duty, to buy in the cheapest market and sell in the dearest" (Essays, 34). The capitalistic counterpart of the medieval attitude lurks outside the sentence, but is not very well concealed; it hangs near the back door in Shaw's statement of what the merchant does *not* plead. The danger of ambiguity prevents him from relying completely on implication.

Or take irony, which I have previously mentioned among the devices of opposition. Of irony in the broad sense—pointing up the disparity between what is and what ought to be—Shaw's prose contains a sufficiency, but it is subsumed under the headings of antithesis and invective. Of irony in the narrower sense— the indirect communication of one's meaning by stating a different one—there is very little in Shaw. He may claim kinship with Swift in sharing that writer's rage over human cruelty and folly, but in satirical method they are scarcely third cousins. When Shaw does fall in ironic step with the reasoning of his opponents, he grows quickly restless, and moves back into his own stride:

The Webbs' arguments and facts were unanswerable: consequently the problem of how not to do it was solved as usual by simply taking no notice of the proposal. (EPWW, 41)

I dislike cruelty, even cruelty to other people, and should therefore like to see all cruel people exterminated. (Too True, 153)

In the first example "consequently" embodies the logic of the do-nothings: when presented with unanswerable facts, ignore

them. But Shaw makes his own stand quite clear, over and
above the irony of the connective, by saying that the problem
was how *not* to do it, and by inserting the contemptuous "as
usual." Nor does the second example play the game of irony
more than halfheartedly. "Even" is the key word; it constitutes
an admission that Shaw is overfastidious in disliking cruelty, and
that his scruples against cruelty to other people are positively
unreasonable—it turns the first part of the sentence into a shy
confession of peculiarity. But the second clause substitutes the
steam roller for the feather duster, leaving no doubt at all of
Shaw's real attitude. The full-blooded ironist must be willing
to leave himself at least slightly open to misunderstanding, say
by very young children and idiots. This risk Shaw is seldom
willing to take—nor is the fact surprising when considered
against the background of his love for exaggeration and his
intolerance of conceptual ambiguity. For such a writer, indirec-
tion becomes almost an intellectual impossibility.

The several ways in which Shaw's style points up antithetical features of experience might have been studied in
Chapter I as evidence of leveling, for the leveler seeks polar-
ities as well as similarities. The impulse toward antithesis can
live peaceably with the habit of equivalence. But on the whole
it seemed best to emphasize the extent to which stylistic oppositions of the Shavian sort fit with his chosen mask, that of the
attacker of received opinion. A good reason for so classifying
his antitheses is that they usually have a strong evaluative slant.
In drawing an antithesis the writer need not invoke values at
all; he may simply make explicit a distinction for its own sake.
But in setting one thing against another Shaw almost invariably
exhibits a preference. His "not_____ but_____" makes a moral

distinction in addition to the conceptual one, and the other forms of antithesis develop contrast so as to cry up one term and cry down the other. If the device were not so admirably suited to Shavian scorn I doubt it would have nearly the prominence in his writing that it does.

4. IDEALISTS AND REALISTS

The role of Cassandra, which Shaw finds congenial in several of his major crusades, entails a particular idea both of reality and of people. The fact that the truth is so apparent to Shaw and so obscure to others presses even his capacious ego to look for some explanation beside the superiority of his intellect. The explanation he seizes on, as I have suggested, is only a slightly less egotistical one: the superiority of his courage in facing facts. Not only in "Common Sense About the War," but in many of his social and critical writings, Shaw strikes the pose of the one uncomfortable realist among a nation of comfortable sentimentalists, and, more bluntly, the one sane man in a nation of fools. The conviction that he alone can and will tell the truth presupposes, thus, a world full of illusions and a populace that resists taking an honest look at that world.

This picture fits with something like schematic rigidity into Shaw's philosophy of Creative Evolution. Within that system man, at present, is a rather primitive experiment of the Life Force, unable to penetrate very deeply the ignorance that shrouds the secrets of life. But evolution is movement in the direction of knowledge. Art and literature, the brightest sparks yet struck by human genius, represent "the struggle of Life to become divinely conscious of itself instead of blindly stumbling hither and thither in the line of least resistance" (M&S, xxiv).

Religion, too, is a step in the direction of awareness, so long as it is not sham religion. Lavinia, the would-be martyr of "Androcles and the Lion," establishes this connection between religion and the striving for truth; a Roman captain accuses her of wanting to die for "Christian fairy stories," and she replies that the approach of death has made her forget the stories, made reality become realer and realer. She is going to die for something greater than stories, but does not yet know what—"If it were for anything small enough to know, it would be too small to die for. I think I'm going to die for God. Nothing else is real enough to die for." The captain asks her what God and she answers, "When we know that, Captain, we shall be gods ourselves" (And, 138–39). Shaw believes that men will become gods, and that divinity will consist mainly in full comprehension of self and reality. Evolution, according to Don Juan, works toward "higher and higher individuals, the ideal individual being omnipotent, omniscient, infallible, and withal completely, unilludedly self-conscious: in short, a god?" (M&S, 112). But at present man is far from godlike in breadth of vision and depth of insight, and the direction of time's arrow—even the fact that it has an arrow—is hidden to all but the scattered men of genius whom the Life Force throws up from time to time as previews of what is to come. Needless to say, Shaw regards himself as one of these evolutionary anachronisms, as a man sitting on the right hand of truth. Hence the role of prophet, and hence the will to do single combat against the hordes of the ignorant. To an advanced thinker like Shaw, most of what other people think is eolithic groping, and must simply be *denied*.

If this notion of the twentieth century as an intellectual Stone Age bears part of the responsibility for the standard

Shavian dichotomy of appearance and reality, a still larger share belongs to the idea that society consciously and unconsciously buries the meat of truth under a crust of lies. Ignorance is deplorable, but hypocrisy is contemptible, and it is hypocrisy, therefore, which most often places Shaw in the position of accuser. He discovered early the deceptions of society, and made them his special target. His novels, the first literary fruits of this revelation, mostly hinge on conflicts between one or more hardheaded characters and a larger number of deluded ones.

The arch-realist Conolly speaks for all of the hard-headed ones in his indictment of polite education:

But what you call her education, as far as I can make it out, appears to have consisted of stuffing her with lies, and making it a point of honor with her to believe them in spite of sense and reason. The sense of duty that rises on that sort of foundation is more mischievous than downright want of principle. I don't dispute your right, you who constitute polite society, to skin over all the ugly facts of life. But to make your daughters believe that the skin covers healthy flesh is a crime. Poor Marian thinks that a room is clean when all the dust is swept out of sight under the furniture; and if honest people rake it out to bring it under the notice of those whose duty it is to remove it, she is disgusted with them, and ten to one accuses them of having made it themselves. She doesn't know what sort of world she is in, thanks to the misrepresentations of those who should have taught her. She will deceive her children in just the same way, if she ever has any. If she had been taught the truth in her own childhood, she would know how to face it, and would be a strong woman as well as an amiable one. But it is too late now. The truth seems natural to a child; but to a grown woman or man, it is a bitter lesson in the learning, though it may be invigorating when it is well mastered. And you know how seldom a hard task forced on an unwilling pupil *is* well mastered. (IK, 253–54)

Shaw's "unpleasant" plays, too, consist mainly in the stripping away of illusions—Trench's illusions about the innocence of interest, the Petkoffs' about war, Morell's about women and marriage, and so on. Mrs. Warren, who has most reason to doubt the saccharine Victorian world-view, gives the lie to society most convincingly, the more so because she is desperately trying to justify herself to her daughter:

You think that people are what they pretend to be—that the way you were taught at school and college to think right and proper is the way things really are. But it's not: it's all only a pretence, to keep the cowardly, slavish, common run of people quiet. . . . The big people, the clever people, the managing people, all know it. They do as I do, and think what I think. (PPU, 1,249)

This is the social alignment against which Shaw sets himself: a few insiders with a gentleman's agreement to keep quiet, and the common run of outsiders, who have no way of disbelieving the lies that are fed them, along with a third group of comfortable middle-class hangers-on, who find it convenient to believe the lies. The poor and the bourgeoisie resemble each other in this respect; both are in darkness as to the real mechanisms of society. "Stupid or comfortably-off" (Essays, 100): these are complementary attributes for Shaw, in that they both lead to falsehood.

His language vividly reflects this preoccupation with lies and deception. A Shaw concordance would show the word "hypocrisy" and its derivatives to have unusual prominence in his vocabulary; one of the worst things he can call a man is hypocrite. A number of similar words are favorites of his too. "Humbug," "sham," "defraud," "pretence," "imposture," "farce," "deception"—these and others are the common coin of Shavian invective. A typical catalogue of sins (scientific sins, in the present instance) lumps "impostures . . . credulities, and delusions . . . brazen lies and priestly pretensions" together with "abominations, quackeries . . . venalities" (Black, lxxxviii). The former group, comprising sins of deception, seems a good deal more vivid.

Aside from the actual labels of hypocrisy, Shaw depends heavily on less direct methods of accusation, such as the opposition of "ostensibly" and an antonym:

ostensibly for a number of capital crimes . . . but essentially for . . . (StJ, 3)

ostensibly a heroic and patriotic defender of his country . . . really an unfortunate man driven by destitution to offer himself as food for powder . . . (Essays, 100)

But such examples carry one back to the realm of style. The point to be made here is that Shaw's contempt for deception hangs like a palpable atmosphere over his writing.

And ultimately, whatever his disgust with lies told to others, his contempt for hypocrisy is greatest when it is directed toward self-deception—if indeed self-deception and deception of others are ever entirely separate. Shaw embraces Ibsenism because he sees in it the exposure of *ideals* to the cold light of day. The idealist hides from fact because he hates himself; the realist sees in ideals "only something to blind us, something to numb us, something to murder self in us, something whereby, instead of resisting death, we can disarm it by committing suicide" (QI, 34). Blindness to reality is spiritual death: the identification of the two is crucial to *The Quintessence of Ibsenism*.

The theme of reality and corrupting ideals counts for much in Shaw's plays, too. One has only to think of Candida, Bluntschli, Caesar, Undershaft, and the like to realize that many Shavian heroes are realists warring genially against the idealists that surround them.[12] And in "Man and Superman" the theme becomes virtually dominant. Don Juan's nickname for Hell is the Palace of Lies, and the main source of his disgust with it is its enthronement of sentimentality and beauty. According to Juan, the earthly ideal of romantic love leads the human will to demand "love, beauty, romance, emotion, passion without their wretched penalties, their expenses, their worries." All this, the Devil answers, is realized here. "Yes, at the cost of death," says Juan (M&S, 121)—Hell is a place where people have died into their irresponsible desires. "Hell is the home of the unreal," Juan says; it differs from earth only in allowing freer license to illusions:

Here you call your appearance beauty, your emotions love, your sentiments heroism, your aspirations virtue, just as you did on earth; but here there are no hard facts to contradict you, no ironic contrast of your needs with your pretensions, no human comedy, nothing but a perpetual romance, a universal melodrama. (M&S, 102–3)

Insofar as one can interpret the third act of "Man and Superman" allegorically, Hell is that condition of the soul which results from living out one's lies; such damnation is the only true death. Don Juan's longest piece of invective catalogues the hypocrisies of the Devil's subjects, and ends with the ultimate accusation, "liars every one of them, to the very backbone of

their souls" (M&S, 129). Briefly, the man who deceives himself
sins against the Life Force. Or, as Shaw puts his case when in
a more pragmatic humor, "If a man cannot look evil in the face
without illusion, he will never know what it really is, or combat
it effectually" (JBOI, 245). The function of ideals and of religions has generally been to sugar-coat conditions that should
be acknowledged and fought; Shaw's mission, as he sees it, is
to write a new mythology that men can believe without such
gross prostitution of the intellect.

If reality is veiled, if Life aspires upward from its present
condition of ignorance to an ultimate condition of knowledge,
if each step in the process involves discarding as obsolete a
once-adequate creed, and if the mass of mankind (particularly
bourgeois mankind) impedes the march toward truth by clinging to its comfortable old deceptions, conscience must cast the
man of genius in the role of opposer. He will be, as Shaw says
of himself, "born mad or a little too sane, his kingdom . . . not
of this world" (Imm, xlvii).

Thus Shaw could excuse Wilde and his like for having
"nothing fundamentally positive to say," because they were "at
least in revolt against falsehood and imposture . . . clearing our
minds of cant, and thereby showing an uneasiness in the presence of error which is the surest symptom of intellectual vitality"
(Back, lxxxiv). The negative mode harmonizes admirably with
the Shavian scheme of things; so much is certain. It would be
unreasonable to ask a more affirmative style from a writer who
finds the world sick, hypocritical, and sinful. But since the habit
of saying No seems to have a life of its own in Shaw's style,
over and above its utility, one may be tempted to ask whether
the Shavian ethic of realism and deception is not child, rather

than parent, to the posture of denial. An emotional complex like negation may well be in some sense more primary in the artist's make-up than a code of beliefs. This is a question that stylistics and criticism must refer to biography and psychology, for it cannot be answered through explication of the text. What critical investigation *can* say is that rhetorical stance and intellectual creed are consonant with one another to a degree that is surely more than chance. Questions of priority aside, the man who thinks Bernard Shaw's thoughts is recognizably the same inner man who favors the rhetoric of opposition.

IV

Social Socialist and
Unphilosophical Philosopher

Intellect is a passion.—"Sham Education"

1. SOCIAL ANATOMY AND THE IMAGINED READER

IT IS no secret that Shaw has ambiguous feelings about democracy. His strange love-hate affair with rule by the masses hangs in suspension between two magnetic poles, distrust of the common man and distrust of the demagogues who are able to wheedle power out of the common man. Shaw settles an uneasy truce with democracy, partly because he does believe society must *serve* everyone equally, and mostly because he cannot think of a smoother transition to socialism, and to a higher stage of evolution. But a "nearly desperate difficulty" with democracy is that "the method of securing it is to give votes to everybody, which is the one certain method of defeating it" (EPWW, 40). In a more flippant vein, he speaks of a "democratic franchise of One Simpleton One Vote" (EPWW, 88). The common man is simply incapable of governing himself, of choosing people who *can* govern him, or even of acquiescing gracefully in good government should it chance to be thrust upon him. He is a stranger to the intellect: "History records very little in the way of mental activity on the part of the mass of mankind except a series of stampedes from affirmative errors into negative ones and back again" (Back, lxxvi). More important still is the fact that the common man is a stranger to *religion*, in the Shavian sense of high passion. Mankind "consists of a huge mass of worldly people and a small percentage of persons deeply interested in religion . . ." (And, 10). This deficiency is the vital one, for it means that the Life Force cannot work through the masses except in the crudest fashion. Incapable of thought, incapable of religion, "the majority . . . is always wrong in its opinion of new developments . . ." (QI, 79).

Thus Shaw never lapses into the socialist's endemic sentimentality, the glorification of the poor. With indisputable logic he points out that if the poor really possessed all the virtues assigned to them we should want to increase their numbers. The poor are *less* good than other people, he is fond of remarking; that is why they should be eliminated. But they do not have the sense to eliminate themselves, and Shaw's hope thus lies with their betters—with the superman, in fact.

Now this formidable personage has always seemed one of Shaw's most unlovely creatures, partly because traces of the superman keep turning up in real-life emperors and dictators, and partly because the superman remains nonetheless a figure of vague and obscure qualities. But though he may be seen as a proto-fascist, it is not hard to put a more favorable construction on him: he is born out of Shaw's sense of the profound differences in ability within the human species, and in his scornful

dissatisfaction with the democratic tendency to produce and ex
alt mediocrity. In spite of this tendency, humanity is capable of
throwing up an occasional genius; why shouldn't it worship,
rather than crucify, these biological sports, and why not ultimately breed from them a majority? Of their present existence
Shaw is the living immodest proof: "I happen to be classed by
the sect of Shavians as a Great Man myself" (EPWW, 337). He
belongs to a natural aristocracy already available to the human
race for its enlightenment and improvement. (One of society's
sins against the Life Force is that it allows such men to remain
childless by making marriage the normal condition of parent-
hood.) But in spite of Shaw's optimism about the likelihood of
lifting the race up by its cerebrum, he anticipates no leveling off
into an equality of greatness: "The rough threefold division into
average, superaverage and subaverage is a natural division, and
will persist in spite of any development of factory legislation or
Socialism" (EPWW, 50). That he should make the division so
neat is characteristic of his predilection for tight categories; that
he should see it as permanent is the predictable result of his belief that the Life Force always gropes restlessly beyond its current level of achievement.

Shaw's three-part anatomy of society has an importance
other than its importance to his social thought. A writer, especially a practical writer who works toward social reform, must
give some consideration to the obscurity into which he casts his
words. Who reads him, and with what insight, what attitudes?
These are questions that Shaw seems concerned with. The first
chapter of *Everybody's Political What's What?* bears the title
"Is Human Nature Incurably Depraved?" and the first sentence
runs, "If it is, reading this book will be a waste of time, and it

should be exchanged at once for a detective story or some pleasant classic, according to your taste." This is an attempt to fix the audience, to establish a minimum shared ground of assumptions upon which to build. In the other major political book, *The Intelligent Woman's Guide*, the title itself specifies the intended audience, and the first chapter goes on to suggest that, although the lady is intelligent, she has read nothing and thought little about socialism, but uncritically accepts the extant social order.

Similarly, a number of the prefaces and major essays begin with some kind of direct address to the reader. The first sentence in *Doctors' Delusions* is: "Please do not class me as one who 'doesn't believe in doctors.'" A sane man urging his sanity on other sane men. The preface to "Androcles and the Lion" begins with a wistful paragraph lamenting the triumph of Barabbas; at the end of it Shaw feels called upon to add, "I am no more a Christian than Pilate was, or you, gentle reader; and yet, like Pilate, I greatly prefer Jesus to Annas and Caiaphas." He goes on to solidify the bond of agnosticism between himself and the reader with "Pray do not at this early point lose patience with me and shut the book. I assure you I am as sceptical and scientific and modern a thinker as you will find anywhere." Other prefaces have titles like "First Aid to Critics" ("Major Barbara") and "Preface for Politicians" ("John Bull's Other Island"). To be sure, most of these attempts to specify an audience and create a particular relationship with it are somewhat less than half serious. Shaw expects men as well as women to read *The Intelligent Woman's Guide* and knows that politicians and critics will make up a minute fraction of the readership of the two prefaces. But such interplay does show him acutely aware of his readers, and anxious to create a fictive setting for the discourse.

This being the case, it is natural that he should often conceive his audience in terms of his segmentation of mankind. A book of his might be picked up by one of the subaverage, the superaverage, or the average (these are categories of ability, not to be confused with the upper, middle, and lower classes). To the subaverage man Shaw, with his scorn for the idols of conventionality, cannot hope to appeal; nor does he consider the subaverage man redeemable. The superaverage man is another story. The more outstanding a man is, the more receptive he is to Shavian iconoclasm, and the more capable he is of digesting Creative Evolution and socialism. But there are drawbacks in making an appeal mainly to the elite. For one thing, the elite are fairly likely to be already on the side of the angels, so that to lecture at them would be superfluous. The great energy Shaw expends prying minds open would be wasted if the minds either were already open or were ready to be opened at the gentlest contact with ideas. For another thing, the superaverage are too rare a species. They may be the custodians of art and culture, but social and religious revolutions need a broader base than they constitute. To the average man, therefore, or at least to the unossified average man, Shaw directs his attention.

For the most part he takes the reader to be a reasonable, fairly intelligent person, possibly quite ignorant of facts, and probably misled by the cant that society doles out as gospel. Such a man can learn, if things are patiently explained to him, and Shaw treats him as a hopeful scholar, though distinctly an inferior in knowledge and sophistication. But there is another important force that impinges on this amiable avuncular relationship: the dead air of subaverage idiocy that surrounds the average man and that, since it is an agreeable enough soporific,

is always threatening to seduce him from the hard path of reason. Shaw really writes with two groups of people in mind, the
audience and the anti-audience; he writes *to* one group, and, as
the last chapter argued, *against* another.

In this battle for the average man's soul, Shaw sometimes
counsels him to feel superior to "Mr. Everybody," whose head
has "a good deal of rubbish" in it (EPWW, 43). He flatters the
average man by contrasting him with the "political five-year-
olds" who will never understand socialism, and "who could not
read this book without falling asleep over its first page" (EP-
WW, 67). He cajoles his reader into assent by setting up categories that the intelligent average man cannot help wanting to
belong to:

no person with the smallest political intelligence is likely to deny that
... (Essays, 152)

a moment's reflection will convince any intelligent person ... (Essays,
189)

The most skeptical scientific reader may therefore ... (StJ, 18)

Nobody who knows ... will doubt ... (StJ, 53)

any properly educated child over the age of six ... (Back, xxxvii)

In reading the last chapter, the intelligent advocate of commercial
enterprise must have ... (Essays, 200)

Or, to reverse this strategy, Shaw may create a class of readers
that the intelligent man will want to *avoid* belonging to: "Of
course it will be said here by incorrigibly slipshod readers that
..." (QI, 131). Sometimes he cautions the intelligent reader
against the arguments of fools: "Any person who, having per-

haps heard that I am a Socialist, attempts to persuade you that
. . . may safely be dismissed from your consideration as an ig-
noramus" (QI, 200). Occasionally he complains to the average
man of the subaverage man's thickness of skull: "You explain to
the working man . . . You buttonhole the shopkeeper . . . It is all
pathetically useless" (Essays, 180–81). Or (to make an end of
this list) he shares with the sensible reader his condescension
toward the subaverage: "I cannot help feeling some compassion
for them when they assure me that . . . The facts are overwhelm-
ingly against them . . . Still, I am sorry for them . . ." (StJ, 55–56).
Once in a while Shaw can be found speaking directly to the subaverage man—one of his radio talks to America begins "Hello
boobs"—but for the most part he leaves the boobs in the background, talking against them but not to them.

    This rather consistent alignment of writer and audience is
interesting for its dependence on Shaw's breakdown of society,
and at least equally interesting for what it reveals about his idea
of the writer's function. There is nothing of the scholar's cell in
his prose; he writes for the forum just as he debated in the
forum. Some writers create a sculptured and polished artifact,
then retreat, leaving it to be admired in its perfection; such
writing is not very personal. But Shaw is a person writing to
real people. He never backs away from his prose, nor does he
modestly allow the reader to take it or leave it, according to
whim. He writes to convince, or, at less serious moments, to agitate, and to these purposes detachment would be fatal. The
average man is salvageable, but not if he is left to his dogmatic
slumbers. He must be shaken, prodded, and nudged into con-
sciousness, and Shaw writes with this end in mind. His prose is
alive with the awareness of audience, as I have suggested. It is

also alive with supposed interchanges between the authorial voice and that audience.

He addresses his reader directly, sometimes apostrophizing him or her by a title—"dear madam" and "intelligent lady" in *The Intelligent Woman's Guide,* "O English reader" in the preface to "John Bull's Other Island"—and frequently using the second-person pronoun. Often, too, he gives instructions and makes requests; the first few chapters of *The Intelligent Woman's Guide* contain a good many. There are direct imperatives: "Do not run to the Socialists . . . Think it out for yourself. Conceive yourself as . . . Beware of such short cuts!" (pp. 12–13). There are softer commands, phrased as requests: "Please do not blame me or throw my book into the fire." (p. 22); "May I call your attention to something that" (p. 45). Sometimes Shaw asks the reader to entertain suppositions: "Suppose the blacksmith swears a good deal, and gets drunk occasionally! . . . Suppose he has what you call an unfortunate manner . . ." (p. 31). He makes concessions ("You can . . ."—p. 32) and commands ("You must . . ."—p. 32) outside the imperative mode. And, also outside the imperative mode, he offers advice: "By the way, you had better leave your own share and that of your children and relations and friends out of the question . . ." (p. 12). Here Shaw favors the tone of gentle command; he maintains a not-quite-patronizing relationship with the reader. Elsewhere the precise tone differs, but it is typical of Shaw to write as if in the presence of a live, responding audience.

A third way, his most common one, of incorporating a reader in the discussion is to ask him questions; the first twenty pages of *The Intelligent Woman's Guide* contain eighteen interrogatives. Of these a few are rhetorical questions in the narrower sense specified by Fowler, questions, that is, to which only one answer is possible, and which are just particularly emphatic forms of statement. When Shaw asks, "How could [St. Paul] help preaching the open mind and the inner light as against all laws and institutions whatever?" (p. 5), he does not seem to pause for an answer. Another question begins, "Are not . . ." (p. 15), a sure sign that its asking is a formality. Such questions do not build a very active relationship between writer and reader, but they do insist that the latter make at least a token response, whereas ordinary assertion may leave the reader passive and uncommitted.

But most of Shaw's questions are rhetorical only in the broader sense of not seeking to elicit information, as a spoken question does. These fall into two groups. One type presumably gives voice to the reader's own puzzlement, anticipating a question that he might ask. The answer, of course, is to be found in the text, frequently right on the heels of the question itself:

What would a teetotaller say if . . . ? He would have a double objection . . . (p. 16)

Why, then, did St Paul give a counsel which . . . ? The explanation is that . . . (p. 4)

Or such queries may set up topics for lengthy discussion: "How much is each of us to have? what is my fair share? what is your fair share? and why?" (p. 21). These are really rhetorical questions in reverse, questions posed *by* the reader *to* the writer. They represent genuine interplay between the two, since with them the writer attempts either to probe his reader's mind for misgivings or to suggest to the reader points on which he *should* be in doubt. The other type of question leads to an even more direct confrontation of writer and reader:

Will you try to make up your mind how you would like to see the income of your country divided up day by day? (p. 12)

What is your own answer? (p. 1)

These are clearly open questions. Shaw himself cannot answer them, nor do they elicit only one possible reply. In fact, they are of a sort not ordinarily found in the written language, outside of personal letters and elementary exercise books, since they seem actually to require a live reply. To call them rhetorical is somewhat misleading, for they constitute one half of an imagined conversation between the writer and the audience, with the audience taking silent but active part.

Imperatives and interrogatives differ formally from declaratives in that a verb precedes any noun in the main clause.[1] They differ semantically from assertions in that they require some kind of response, either verbal or nonverbal. Failing to make such a response is an impolite act, according to the rules of conversation and conduct, for these "request utterances" (as they are sometimes called) represent an effort on the speaker's part to elicit behavior from his hearer. The audience participation they demand can never occur under the eyes of the writer, and perhaps for this reason he does not usually employ them, at least not in formal discourse. If he does use a number of them he shows an especially vivid awareness of his unseen audience and a strong desire to offer that audience an explicit intellectual challenge. Shaw's taste for request utterances[2] is a sign of the extent to which he writes as if he were speaking, and speaking to real human beings. Moreover, as I have suggested, he writes to human beings of a fairly well-defined class, whose qualities of mind distinguish them from other classes among whom it would be a waste of time to proselytize. Shaw writes *personal* prose, not in the sense of committing his intimate secrets to paper, but in the sense of postulating a real audience and speaking to that audience with a live and recognizable voice.

2. THE UNIVERSE AS HUMANIST

Shaw the personal writer has his counterpart in Shaw the philosopher. But the connection may seem tenuous, and a closer look at his thought than I have yet taken is in order here.

The philosopher is not the most ingratiating of Shaw's roles, nor is Creative Evolution the most appealing of his ideas. He puts off some readers with his truculent mysticism, others with his claim to have formulated the religion of the future, others with his antiscientism, still others with his dogmatism. As a result many of his admirers have turned away from Creative Evolution in bewilderment or annoyance, and concluded that it is a kind of useless appendage to Shaw's socialism or an unimportant consequence of his skepticism as to conventional religion. Other admirers (Joad, for instance) have not been alienated by Shaw's aspirations to philosophy, but have taken them seriously and sought to systematize his beliefs. Both reactions are unfortunate, I think. His beliefs will scarcely bear systematizing—to do so is to strip them of their vitality as well as of their plausibility—and both philosophers and scientists have pretty generally agreed to ignore Shaw's contributions. But in spite of this cool professional reception, students of his drama and his social thought should not ignore or dismiss his philosophy. Shaw is too intense a thinker, too committed to his work, to have taken solace in a detachable or irrelevant religion, whatever the capricious arguments he sometimes uses to defend it. Creative Evolution springs from deep sources in his intellect, not from the tyro's wish to "have" a philosophy.

The world can be seen as permutations of matter, swirled about according to immutable laws. This view, as I have shown (Chapter I), is repugnant to Shaw. For one thing it slights energy, by which he is greatly impressed: he calls Beethoven great because his music anticipated the concept of nuclear energy, of a vital force that informs even the minutest particles of matter. "Energy," "force," "vitalism"—all are plus-words for Shaw, who praises both metaphysical and physical "overcomers of inertia" (Back, lxxxii). But even more crucial to his rejection of mechanism is the horror of determinism, the coin whose other side is *chance*. A science that makes an idol of chance is an irrational science, Shaw claims. And those who admit a vital force but make it just one of many material forces go only halfway toward a mature view. The full-blooded vitalists are possessed by a "divine idea of the life breathed into the clay nostrils of Adam," and filled by their researches "with a sense of the miraculousness of life" (Back, lxxiii). There is matter on the one hand, and on the other hand there is vitality. Driven by a feeling that life runs on a different schedule than does inert matter, Shaw posits a twofold order of things, the physical and the metaphysical. He seeks always to find the "spiritual realities behind material facts" (QI, 55), imitating in this his master, Samuel Butler.

In spite of his animadversions against science for its irrationality, Shaw is himself forced into recognition—almost into worship—of an irrational element in the universe, by the conviction that life is "the satisfaction of a passion in us of which we can give no rational account whatever" (QI, 324). If the order of nature is apart from the order of grace, then the disciplines that study the one—science—will be inadequate to the other. "Every genuine scientist must be, finally, a metaphysician" (Back, lxxiii), says Shaw, or fall short of real insight into the workings of things. Hence the failure of Darwinism as a world view. Shaw's grudge against noncreative evolution is a reaction to its very partial account of progress, and to its enmity toward all religion, Shavian as well as conventional. "Religion" is one of those words that he uses in two opposite senses: traditional religion is a hodgepodge of fairy tales that the nineteenth century did well to purge itself of; but in doing so it blinded itself to genuine religion, which human existence must feed on. Shakespeare is great, in spite of his lack of religion, only because he "had religion enough to be aware that his religionless condition was one of despair" (Back, lxxxv). For Shaw, art is essentially religious activity; the very greatest of artists (Michelangelo, Beethoven, Goethe) build their work on a metaphysic just as surely as Bergson does. They move in a region where science cannot of its own force enter, the region of the Holy Ghost, whose apostle Shaw repeatedly declares himself to be.

One of the consequences of his accepting a dichotomy of matter and spirit is his optimism; or should one say rather that his optimism entails his metaphysic? Whatever the priority, the two are closely related. Chance might buffet the world now toward chaos, now toward order, but with the Life Force in charge the ultimate direction of things can only be toward a tidy universe. Thus in "The Sanity of Art" Shaw attacks Nordau's *Degeneration* because it sees society as sinking into disorder and art as hastening the decline. For Shaw, art is the *avant-garde* of human thought in its upward progress: "The great artist is he who . . . by supplying works of a higher beauty and a higher interest than have yet been perceived, succeeds, after a brief struggle with its strangeness, in adding this fresh extension of sense to the heritage of the race" (QI, 329). Hence the privileged state of art, and hence Shaw's lifelong battle against censorship. A church, a state, or an orthodoxy of any sort must either believe that freethinkers will settle eventually on its doctrines, or it must admit that it has no faith in those doctrines (StJ, 36). The climax of free, human, mental process will inevitably be truth, as that of evolution will be mastery of environment.

Shaw takes the stuff of human beings as infinitely pliable clay, given time enough for molding. One of our "superstitions," according to him, is "that human nature cannot be changed (although changeability is one of the recognized qualities of human nature)" (Essays, 324; and see EPWW, 59). In Chapter II, I discussed Shaw's receptiveness to change in institutions and traditions. One thing that permits him to be so sanguine about an economic and social housecleaning is his double faith, that human nature will yield to pressure from outside, and that in the long run it can even be made to transcend itself. In human development, as in evolutionary history, "life continues thrusting toward higher and higher organization . . ." (QI, 202).

This quotation gets at the heart of the matter, in both wording and syntax. *Life* is an active agent, not a passive receiver of form. It has, seemingly, a will of its own, and power to implement that will. In Shaw's dichotomy of mind and matter, mind has the upper hand, since only that which is vital can serve as a *cause.* Thus he echoes Butler, complaining that Darwinism implies the "banishment of mind from the universe." (Back, xlviii), and he shudders at the "unspeakable horror of the mindless, purposeless world" (PP&R, 70). Such a world not only grates against Shaw's preferences, but displeases him as a scientific theory, too. Darwinism posits evolutionary machinery that is hopelessly inadequate as an explanation for the upward movement that Shaw sees in nature: evolution is the working of the Holy Ghost in things, for only such a supernatural driving force could lead to such satisfactory shaping of matter.

Shaw is a practical thinker, and he anchors his metaphysic of the Life Force in observations of human conduct. Around him he sees women endowed with a mating instinct much more convincing than the lip service of the Victorians to sexual propriety. He finds artists imaging life in original and superior ways. He discovers social prophets (Jesus or Joan of Arc, for example) voicing doctrine for which there is no parentage in their milieu, hundreds or thousands of years before the average mind is ready to receive it. Such anomalies seem to him inexplicable by the ordinary laws of history, so he takes them as evidence of an extramaterial force. The point of tangency between the metaphysical and the physical is in such people; spirit may be the first cause, but it works through human decisions, human character. In most men the vital force is weak. In some it is strong but misdirected into the pursuit of shabby crusades; but the achievement of a few redeems this enormous waste.

However antisocial these few may seem to the majority, the Life Force is ultimately pro-social. Politicians may mouth platitudes about the unwillingness of Britons to be slaves, but what really leads to the gradual increase of freedom is "the divine sense that liberty is a need vital to human *growth*" (Back, lxvii; italics mine). Thus a spiritual force moves ordinary people in spite of their dwelling beneath the plane of greatness. Protestantism's pursuit of the inner light is just one phase of the "sweet" tradition that "good people follow a light that shines within and above and ahead of them, that bad people care only for themselves, and that the good are saved and blessed and the bad damned and miserable" (Back, lxxiv). Morality, in the good sense, has no absolute goal—thus Shaw's rejection of various ideals that claim permanent validity in moral codes—but moves with the Life Force toward a more abundant existence, against the wishes of the masses but to their great benefit. We do not live for reasons, Shaw says, but in "fulfilment of our will to live" (QI, 23), and the will to live can only be a prosocial force in the long run.

It is significant that even his most systematic statement of all this, the preface to "Back to Methuselah," lacks anything resembling philosophic rigor, and that both before and after writing this bible of Creative Evolution (1921) Shaw is gaily eclectic in filling out his world picture. That he treats it as only a rude preliminary draft of a new iconography reflects his preoccupation with a few overwhelming attitudes rather than with systematic completeness. Those attitudes are the important thing, and they can be summed up under the single heading of *anthropocentrism*.

The Life Force may not be a kindly old man with a beard —it is not *anthropomorphic*—but it does think with a human brain, seek human goals, and work through human action. Shaw likes the idea of a universe becoming more and more congenial to people, evolving into their desires, submitting increasingly to

their control. In this Bergsonian, vitalistic world, mind is supreme. It controls all process and seems even to be the end of
process: the wise ancients in the last play of "Back to Methuselah" look forward to the total autonomy of mind, and Lilith's
concluding speech lauds "the goal of redemption from the flesh
. . . the vortex freed from matter . . . the whirlpool in pure intelligence."[3] (Back, 261). A much younger Shaw, preoccupied
with problems of morality, had already hit on the idea: the
"pure law of thought" (QI, 186), he said, is the law of God-
head, which only compromises temporarily with stupidity by
relying on the impure law of commandments. Shaw is too much
oriented toward human beings and their shifting needs to stake
his total commitment on any fixed morality or any philosophical
system. Men, not ideas, are the important thing, since ideas are
merely the artifacts of mind, which is the constantly improving
servant of living men.

Shaw's convictions as to the importance of human will and
mind lead him into some strange byways. He sometimes talks,
if only as a *façon de parler*, as though lower organisms in the
evolutionary scale were masters of their development, as if the
giraffe grew a longer neck by trying to do so. Another example
is his exaggerated antipathy toward Freudian psychology (although he hopes for much from psychology in general). He deplores the "morbidities of psycho-analysis" (IWG, 470) in its
"grotesque Freudian beginnings" (IWG, 466), because, one
surmises, of the irrationality of sexual repression and the idea
that man is slave to impulses he cannot control with the conscious mind. Similarly, his doctrinaire abstinence from drink
stems at least partly from a dread of relinquishing mental control over the body. Captain Shotover speaks for his creator when

he says, "To be drunk means to have dreams; to go soft, to be
easily pleased and deceived . . ." (HH, 119). More importantly,
his exaltation of mind leads to his exaltation of power by a direct route. As Don Juan puts it, "To be in hell is to drift: to be
in heaven is to steer" (M&S, 134). Rational man is in control of
himself; thus Shaw's horror of determinism, and his gravitation
toward its antipode, the heroism of the great man. The quickest
road to the superman is through his present-day forebears, who
must have power in order to impose their superior vision on
ordinary men. Thus Cusins, after his conversion to Undershaft-
ism, thinks that "all power is spiritual," and that power for evil
is an unfortunate but necessary concomitant of power for good
(JBOI, 346). Shaw's vegetarianism and antivivisectionism also
mesh with his projection of human mentality into every corner
of the world. His excessively delicate sympathy for dumb creatures is the natural consequence of belief in a chain of being
whose links are welded together by mind.

But if Shaw's anthropocentric doctrine has in it some pockets of eccentricity, and if it falls short of scientific or philosophic
rigor, it is at least good humanism, and he a good humanist. His
socialism springs from humane attitudes: distaste for exploita-
tion of one man by another; concern for the suffering of the
poor and, more important, for the cramping of the human spirit
by social limitations; impatience with the inefficient flounder-
ing of a chance-ridden society; aspiration toward improvement
of the breed. And when he espouses antihumanistic policies,
such as extermination of the incorrigible criminal and steriliza-
tion of the yahoo, he does so out of a larger humanism that prefers the good of the whole race to the unlimited license of individuals. To Shaw, Dean Inge's "supreme heresy" is the

denunciation of "anthropolatry" (PP&R, 167). The impetus of such a humanism can, to be sure, carry a thinker past controlled and rational democracy and into totalitarianism, but, whatever his theoretical pronouncements, Shaw always stopped short of this practical extreme. His humanism grows out of a sincere regard for people, not out of a set of theories.

Like his unsocial socialist, Sidney Trefusis, Shaw the man had rough edges and prickles that made him hard for society to digest. His insulting manner, his refusal to take part in small talk and frivolous socializing, his odd clothes, his vitriolic criticism of the arts, his impatience with mediocrity, and his public egotism, all smack of misanthropy. But like Trefusis, who in spite of the stern face he presents to society, shows a deeper gentleness by financing emigration for deserving workmen, and even bringing harmony into a dissonant romance, Shaw has no personal bite behind his doctrinal bark. To be flayed by Shaw in a controversy never entails being cut by him personally. A curious thing about Shaw is the way his enemies tend to become (or remain) his friends: warmth of friendship succeeds warmth of invective between him and Max Nordau, Henry Arthur Jones, H. G. Wells, Dean Inge, G. K. Chesterton. The latter said that it was always an ennobling experience to argue with Shaw; if so, part of the reason was doubtless the intellectuality of Shaw's passion and the impersonality of his rancor. Toward other men he feels (along with impatience) profound interest and genuine compassion—the more genuine because it takes the form, not of idly sentimentalizing the masses, but of arduously acting in their favor. Shaw would perhaps not care enough about mind to project its working into the workings of Nature if he did not also care enough about human beings to take on the responsibility of ministering to individual minds that he considers diseased.

3. IDEAS AND MEN

That this humanist's concern extends to Shaw's style in the form of a lively interplay between author and audience I tried to demonstrate in the first section of this chapter. He writes *to* one set of people and *against* another set, so that his prose is personal in an important sense. It is also personal in the more bizarre sense of being about people—a claim that I propose to substantiate in this section by citing both some extremely obvious evidence and some that is not at all obvious.

But first let me anticipate an objection: naturally his writing is about people, it might be argued; for he is primarily an imaginative writer who, when he turns to discursive prose, carries with him the dramatist's penchant for creating and manipulating characters. This line of reasoning does not impress me. In the first place, Shaw is "primarily" a dramatist only in that he is best known as one. He wrote scarcely anything but novels, essays, and tracts before he was forty, and he remained a prolific essayist after his success on the stage. All told, he wrote many more pages of prose than of drama. For another thing, even if one invokes the spirit of the playwright to interpret the prose of the essayist, one needs an explanation of Shaw's having gravitated toward the drama in the first place. So I prefer to explain the personal content of his prose as *sui generis*, though related to the personal emphasis in all of his thought and artistic activity.

One more disclaimer: when I say he writes about people I do not mean that in the most trivial way; the proportion of strictly biographical writing in the corpus of his work is not particularly large. In the course of his prefaces he is led naturally into biographical sections on Joan of Arc, Jesus, St. Paul, Shakespeare, and others. Often he talks about his own life. But his books and most of his major prefaces are in no sense biographies. The human content of his prose enters by various side doors, and this fact makes it especially significant.

To begin with, when Shaw confronts the anti-audience an obvious result is argument. The pages of his books ring with debate, one-sided though the arguments may be (see Chapter III). Nor does he limit such dialectic to himself and the anti-audience. Fictitious debates among parties of the third, fourth, and fifth parts fill the courtroom of his prose. If one has to point to a *dramatic* element in his style, surely it is this tendency to assign each point of view to an imaginary speaker or to a disembodied voice. Thus, when Shaw outlines seven ways of distributing wealth he does not mechanically list them as possible procedures; he sets up hypothetical partisan groups to propose them. He introduces the first procedure with "a plan which has often been proposed . . ." and goes on to say that this particular plan is the one that workers advocate. He continues, "Others say . . . Some believe in . . . Some say . . . Some say . . . Others say simply . . . What the Socialists say is that none of these plans will work very well, and that . . ." (IWG, 21). These are real programs supported by live people, and Shaw's prose acknowledges that fact by keeping a company of speakers in the wings, ready to come onstage and voice one or another point of view.

Often they do not merely speak and then depart, but stay to conduct a dialogue, monitored by Shaw. At another point in

The Intelligent Woman's Guide (pp. 405–6) he is speculating on the possible necessity of backing up the child's morality with tales of an omniscient enforcer. The mother may (he tells her) merely manufacture pragmatic reasons for good conduct: "You can say 'If I catch you doing that again I will . . .' " But threats only breed cunning. On the other hand, the mother may tell the child that God is always looking, and will punish the child after death. Here the dialogue begins. Shaw postulates a "matter-of-fact" child, who answers the accusation of sin with "What then? What is sin?" The mother may answer "Have you no conscience, child?" but the child replies, "What is conscience?" And so on. Shaw suggests to the mother several more lines of reproach, and predicts the results. Now "debate" may be too pretentious a word for this; the point is merely that it brings his characters into the foreground and lets them talk, rather than submerging them in abstract and impersonal theorizing about their conduct.

Most often, to be sure, the give and take is not restricted to the puppets, but takes place between one or more of them and the authorial voice. Shaw mentions their beliefs or statements in order to refute or accept them, so that at times his posture resembles that of a judge to whom contentions are submissively referred for arbitration. With magisterial confidence he deals out favorable or unfavorable comment. As an example, consider two paragraphs from Shaw's discussion of the population question (IWG, 100–102); in it he handles thirteen propositions as follows:

need we doubt that . . .

It is certain that . . .

The people who say that . . . are only pretending to understand it.

If the Socialists were to say   they would be equally pretending to understand it.

The sensible course is to . . . or, as some would say, trust in God that evil will not come out of good.

it would be ridiculous to refrain from . . . on the ground that . . .

We should never do anything at all if we listened to the people who tell us that the sun is cooling . . .

It would be quite sensible to say "Let us . . ." if . . .

It would be foolish anyhow to say ". . ."

It is just like saying ". . ." as lazy people do . . .

Note that . . . the earth is said by the political economists to be . . .

If any gentleman tries to persuade you that . . . you may safely conclude that he has been told to say so at a university for the sons of the rich. . . .

who would like you to believe that . . .

Snaking his way among so many ideas, claims, and statements, Shaw lets his syntax get rather complex: on this page there are thirty-five dependent clauses, not to mention infinitive phrases and co-ordinate clauses; and though this total is unusually high, a large amount of subordination is common in his writing.[4]

Another predictable form taken by these inlays of prefabricated statements is the quotation, of which a large number punctuate his discourse. In five pages of "Common Sense About the War" (39–43) there are twelve direct quotations, one of them a page long. They belong to one consecutive, loosely strung discussion, but it is a hypothetical one, not a sequence of

speeches recorded from life. Shaw assigns the first two quotations to "the Junkers of all nations," the next to Sazanoff, Russian Secretary for Foreign Affairs, the next to Sir Edward Grey,
then another one to Sazanoff. Other disputants: the Pope, Grey
again, Sazanoff again, the Kaiser, the Germans (twice), and
Grey a third time. Almost all of these speeches are Shaw's ren-
ditions, not actual quotations; they witness no scholarly defer-
ence to source material, but comprise a live reconstruction of
debate that took place only figuratively. In addition to the direct quotations, there are roughly sixteen indirect ones. This
passage is admittedly more packed with dialogue than the
norm, since Shaw is tracing an actual series of historical events.
But the generalization applies throughout his prose: he is a
good deal more fond of parceling out lines to imaginary or real
speakers than are most writers.[5]

Quotation marks signal direct quotation. The commonest
mark of indirect discourse is a locution I shall call the introductory "that," to distinguish it from the demonstrative and
from the relative pronoun. It is introductory in that it leads into
the words assigned to someone else. In Shaw's heavily popu-
lated intellectual world indirect quotation abounds even more
than direct. He is constantly reporting what so-and-so says or
believes or holds or denies or knows, and in order to do so
without setting the proposition inside quotation marks he must
use the introductory "that." Trivially, he uses it to report
speeches of real people ("Florence Nightingale said bluntly
that . . ."—Dilemma, 23) or hypothetical speeches of imagined
people ("No burglar contends that . . ."—Dilemma, 49). But
even more often he uses it to report the mental processes of his
puppets:

Utopians must not conclude that . . . (EPWW, 48)
Mussolini, banking on his belief that . . . (Essays, 321)
people who conceive that . . . (JBOI, 230)

Or he uses it merely to mention propositions, not that somebody holds, but that *nobody* in a certain group holds; this is a
device especially typical of his rhetorical questions:

can any of the modern substitutes for the Inquisition . . . claim that
. . .? (StJ, 42)

does anyone who . . . has studied history . . . believe that . . .? (3PP,
209)

What sane commercialist would decree that . . .? (Back, lxxix)

And frequently the proposition introduced by "that" floats free
from any specific asserter, though somebody does apparently
believe it:

It may be argued that . . . (Essays, 194)
It is easy to say that . . . (Essays, 205)
It will be at once seen that . . . (Essays, 40)
I find . . . a strong conviction that . . . (3PP, 208)

Some of these forms refer to beliefs that anyone at all might
hold, some to beliefs of audience and anti-audience, and some
to beliefs that have no visible proprietors at all. Occasionally
"that" prefaces a proposition that is attributed to a non-human
agent, as when words or events "*mean* that . . . ." However shad-
owy the speaker behind the assertion, these constructions are
important evidence that Shaw intrudes into his prose other
voices than his own. More than other writers he moves in a
realm of propositions, and, whether or not he assigns them to

particular or visible speakers and believers, they evoke the atmosphere of the forum rather than that of the study.

It is interesting to note that these constructions fall into a neatly defined grammatical class, a subgroup of the "factive nominals." Formally, these nominals are derived by including a declarative sentence within another sentence (of any type), where the included sentence then functions as a noun. Robert B. Lees, in the best treatment of English nominalizations,[6] semantically distinguishes "that" clauses from other nominals by saying that they refer to *facts* or *statements*, rather than to actions or events: that is, they deal with experience, not directly, but indirectly, through the form of a proposition. This analysis supports my contention that Shaw's heavy reliance on these forms indicates a peculiarly verbal or dramatic emphasis in his prose.

This holds true, because of the grammatical form and its semantic force, even when his "that" clauses treat propositions abstractly, independent of their being actually or possibly entertained by anyone. When a writer mentions a proposition in this way, he usually does so in order to weigh it as a claimant to credence, to condition the reader's attitude toward it, to accept or reject it. Shaw evaluates propositions in a variety of ways using the introductory "that," often in conjunction with the expletive "it":

it is not yet clear that . . . (Essays, 194)

It goes without saying that . . . (Essays, 310)

It is a mistake to suppose that . . . (3PP, 203)

It is equally easy and equally absurd to say that . . . (Essays, 205)

it is the chief and overwhelming advantage of public enterprise that
. . . (Essays, 200)

The moral is that . . . (Essays, 245)

That . . . is natural enough (StJ, 27)

The obvious fact that . . . (Essays, 276)

To *mention* a proposition without asserting it might seem
a way to stand back and leave the reader free to make his own
evaluation, but Shaw precludes this possibility; he seldom lets
a proposition slip by without attempting either to commend it
or damn it. Thus, even though these forms do not necessarily
suggest debate, Shaw makes them do so by adding the requisite
second voice—his own—with a running commentary on the
core propositions. Constructions involving the introductory
"that," especially in his hands, bring the human mind into the
foreground, both because a proposition normally implies someone to entertain it, and because it invites the author's judgment
as well as the reader's. Indirect discourse, to speak metaphorically, splits the writer's personality; it divides the authorial voice
into two voices. Instead of merely making a point, Shaw *refers
to* a point as if someone else had made it, then comments on it.
The complexity added by such bifurcation is essentially a human complexity, in that it involves counterpointing of voices
and minds. Writing about propositions is an indirect way of
writing about people.

The pressure of Shaw's interest in attaching ideas to believers or deniers is probably responsible for his frequent use
of the introductory "that."[7] To take an example, two pages of
the preface to "The Doctor's Dilemma" (xxviii–xxix) yield
twelve repetitions of the construction:

it was plain that . . .	concluding that . . .
also evident that . . .	was assumed that . . .
does not follow that . . .	do not suggest that . . .
said bluntly that . . .	fact remains that . . .
did not know that . . .	the assumption that . . .
deny that . . .	the objection that . . .
and that . . .	

In addition to these locutions the same two pages contain numerous other references to propositions, beliefs, attitudes, and so forth. Fifteen are fairly clearly identifiable:

she was snubbed as . . .	proposition
this was the line taken	no more dreamt of . . . being . . .
ardor of conviction	Sydenham dreamt of . . . being . . .
theory	deny
by simply calling . . .	defend
accuse their patient . . . of	denounce
deny	objection
affirm	

The total is impressive, and not especially unusual for Shaw.[8] His ambiance is one of disputatious voices, conflicting ideas, acceptable and unacceptable notions, trustworthy and untrustworthy advocates.

An even clearer measure of the human content in Shaw's prose is the way he draws on men's actions and attitudes to illustrate points he is making. For him, ideas merit attention mainly because they affect people (as we shall see later), and therefore he seldom carries on an argument for long without reducing its terms to the lowest common denominator in human experience. Richness of illustration is one thing that makes his writing so interesting.

Take as an example a letter he wrote to *The Sunday Express* on vivisection (Delusions, 138–46). His intention is to refute a letter from H. G. Wells, in which Wells exonerates the vivisector on the ground that knowledge is an end that justifies almost any means—exactly the kind of abstract reasoning that Shaw disapproves of. He answers Wells not with a counter-absolute but with a barrage of examples: the vivisector who will not cease his inquiries into the gustatory properties of roast baby (Shaw is thinking of Swift's "Modest Proposal") until he has gone on to sample boiled, fried, and fricasseed baby as well, all in the interests of abstract knowledge; a "gentleman" who sought to find out how long he could keep a dog's confidence if he chopped off one of its paws whenever it approached affectionately; Joseph Lister, who poured boiling water on frogs and defended such practices against Queen Victoria's strictures; Landru and Smith, famous wife-murderers, who at least "had not the effrontery" to argue as Wells does; Galileo dropping cannon balls from the tower of Pisa, but refraining from using lightweight and heavyweight boxers; experimenters who spend fabulous sums giving cancer to mice and "developing in themselves the mouse mind"; Dr. Hadwen, an opponent of vivisection who won a famous court case and showed public opinion to be on his side; and St. Thomas the doubter, who by thrusting his hands into Christ's wounds in order to establish his existence showed what a sound vivisector he would have made. Such illustration exposes the absurdity of an idea by fleshing out its abstractions. All of Shaw's examples here introduce live experimenters, real imbecility, and real suffering into an argument about knowledge and pain, which Shaw refuses to divorce from individuals who know and creatures that feel pain.

These individuals do not always appear in three-dimensional detail, of course; often they appear under generic names that assign them only one quality: "the man who . . ." or "the laborer." Thus in three pages of *The Intelligent Woman's Guide* Shaw gives us the following cast of characters: "a sempstress," "a famous opera singer," "a laborer to chop wood," "a popular actress," "a famous surgeon," "a famous barrister," "a child with an interesting face and pretty ways, and some talent for acting," "a pretty girl . . . her plain sister," "a skilled workman," "a clever woman," "a village carpenter," "the farmer," "a village boy," "the postman," "the policeman," "the doctor," "a clergyman," "the member of Parliament," "the domestic servant," "the Queen or King," "an actor," "the housemaid," "the shop assistant," "a blacksmith, carpenter, or builder," "a man of business" (pp. 24–26). But though these worthies have only the sketchiest outlines, they bring life to Shaw's writing much more than is normal in the pages of economics. It is doubtful that Shaw would be interested in the dismal science at all were he not able to conceive supply and demand in terms of sempstresses and woodchoppers.

Nothing is more suggestive of this ability to link ideas with men than his frequent reference to himself, one of the grounds on which he is accused of egotism. If he had written no essays explicitly about himself, and left no letters, it would be easy to compile a fairly large (if not necessarily accurate or complete) biography solely from incidental autobiographical remarks. The preface to "Back to Methuselah" is in part a Shavian *Bildungsroman*. From the preface to "The Shewing-Up of Blanco Posnet" one learns about Shaw's part in the controversy over censorship. The preface to *Immaturity* describes his family and upbringing.

The preface to *The Irrational Knot* narrates his youthful efforts to crash London's literary gates. In his essays on medicine he reveals, among other things, a good deal about his own medical history.[9] Egotism this certainly is. But a more generous and equally accurate interpretation can be arrived at by taking the wealth of personal allusion as a sign of Shaw's involvement in his material, his sense of the relevance of ideas to conduct and experience.

His peculiar brand of humanism has some more insignificant, though interesting, by-products in his style. A curious one is the predominance of the human body in his imagery. Shaw is not a highly figurative writer, so it is the more surprising to find him drawing heavily on any one source of images. Disease is a particular favorite of his. He often establishes figurative links between social or moral disorders on the one hand and physical disorders on the other. The war is a pestilence resulting from shoddy political hygiene (HH, 7). A conquered nation—Ireland, specifically—is like a man with cancer (JBOI, 40). Sudden nationalization of industry without compensation is catastrophic because "the patient [i.e., the economy] dies before the remedy has time to operate" (IWG, 316). Shaw speaks of a bad conscience "quite as uncomfortable as a bad cold" (Delusions, 213), of "disuse of the moral muscles" (JBOI, 48), and of "a blind spot on [officers'] moral retina" (JBOI, 47). The fact that these tropes are unelaborate is rather in support of my point than not. An extended metaphor is a conscious artistic effort and may be quite atypical in its icon, but these casual forays into imagery show how close at hand their substance must be.

Imagery is a small matter in Shaw's style. A much more adequate index to his traffic with people and events is the number of proper names that fill his pages.[10] To use one of these names is usually to specify a one-member class, whereas other nouns have many referents and depend for specificity on the context. Names do not have meanings in the ordinary sense: they are more like signs than like symbols. Their interpretation depends relatively little on interaction with other words, and relatively much on the interpreter's rote knowledge of certain parts of the external world. Especially, they point to those segments of the extralinguistic world that are important enough to men to have been assigned private linguistic categories. Through them Shaw reaches out into public affairs quite often —thirty-six times on one not too unusual page in the preface to "The Millionairess" (Simp, 112):

Napoleon (three times)	Rome	Somme
Cromwell (three times)	Dunbar	Nelson
Wellington (three times)	Waterloo	British
Caesar (twice)	Ludendorff	Dardanelles
Marlborough (twice)	Haig	War Office
Pharsalia (twice)	Chicago	Hastings
Saxe	Irish	Mussolini
Shah of Iran	Vinegar Hill	Hitler
Riza Khan	Marengo	Kemal

Though the passage is specifically about great men and wars, the trait is a typical Shavian one. It was with real regret that he wrote Sidney Webb (in 1945), "I forget names so desperately— even Napoleon and Shakespear have become uncertain—that when I write history I have to do it with an encyclopedia at my elbow."[11] Not just when he writes history, but generally, he maintains an intimate relationship between ideas and human action.

A slight shift in choice of evidence produces another interesting count: the number of proper names, personal pronouns,
and words for which personal pronouns might be substituted.
This total is a fairly direct measure of reference to people, and
as might be expected Shaw scores relatively high on it.[12] On
two pages taken at random there are twenty-three and forty
words of this category (Dilemma, 29–30). Equally significant
is the fact that such words constitute over 50 per cent of Shaw's
grammatical subjects, even though he seldom writes straight
history or biography.[13] It needs little interpretation of these
statistics to show that Shaw occupies himself especially with
human beings, that he does not discuss his favorite ideas without constant allusion to their human relevance.

Another point of intersection in his prose between ideas
and people lies in his treatment of causation and logical implication. According to Jean Piaget[14] the child's various "whys"
radiate from a common source: concern with psychological motivation. In the child's animistic universe all causal interaction
is seen in the light of purpose and intention, as if processes oc-
curred only at the bidding of mind. A large number of his
"whys" seek a motivation for natural happenings that the adult
would probably not question at all and certainly would not
attribute to someone's intention. An even larger number of the
child's "whys" refer directly to human behavior. Without implying that Shaw's mind functions in a childlike fashion, it is
interesting to note that the overwhelming majority of his causal
connections have to do in one way or another with human
thought and conduct, the very root of our notion of causation.

A good example is his characteristic use of the word "if."
Sometimes the "if" clause explicitly states the motive for doing
a thing mentioned in the main clause:

if your only object is to . . . then you need give no more than . . . (And, 59–60)

If anyone doubts this, let him . . . (StJ, 19)

If you dispute its justice, state . . . (And, 57)

Frequently the "if" clause suggests a set of psychological conditions and the main clause deals with the psychological consequences: "If you consider their class interests . . . you will understand why Ricardo . . . never dreamt of . . ." (Essays, 41). The sentence explains not only the mental processes of the reader, but those imputed to Ricardo as well. Similarly, "If we have to take thought for the morrow . . . it will be impossible for us to think of nobler things . . ." (And, 58). Though these conditional sentences deal with one person's motivation, many others involve psychological interaction of two or more people:

If we ask our stockbroker . . . he will reply . . . (And, 52)

If we urge a rich man to sell . . . he will . . . (And, 52)

if you venture to wonder how . . . you will produce an extraordinary dismay . . . (And, 49)

Or, finally, Shaw uses the "if" clause as a vehicle for considerations that lead to a value judgment in the main clause, as when he says that "if we feel anything less than acute disappointment" at the present impossibility of socialism, "our institutions have corrupted us . . ." (Essays, 63). These are all, in one way or another, "ifs" of motivation. They exhibit Shaw concerning himself, not with physical events and causes, but with human beings and motives, in a way that (Piaget's work suggests) is deeply natural to the human intellect.

Naturally the key word need not be "if," though it is one of Shaw's favorites. But whether the causal marker is a participle ("A genius is a person who, *seeing* farther and *probing* deeper than other people, has a different set of ethical valuations . . ."— StJ, 7), a subordinating conjunction ("I greatly shocked a . . . newspaper . . . *because* . . ."—And, 73), a conjunctive adverb ("It would *therefore* be a waste of time now to . . ."—StJ, 7), (italics mine throughout), or some subtler combination of words, it usually signals a relationship of necessity involving motivation. The causal nexus for Shaw is a nexus between one person and another, between thought and deed or thought and thought, between fact and attitude. That so many of his causal links are of this sort [15] fits well with the exalted position he gives to mind in the universe. Instead of stressing physical process he stresses, whenever possible, either mental process or the instigators and observers of physical process. Psychological causation, the first area in which the child's causal sense awakens, may remain for the adult a focal point of causal inquiry, especially if he has, like Shaw, an antimechanistic bias.

Mind and action meet in causal locutions; they are also conjoined stylistically in the infinitive form, "to____," which Shaw uses with relatively high frequency.[16] That this form is related to the others I have been discussing may seem strange, but a glance at a few infinitives will show the connection. The infinitive refers to an action, broadly construed, and the words immediately preceding it often evaluate that action or reveal the writer's attitude toward it:

it is foolish to wait . . .
the only sane course is to take . . .
there is no reason to suppose . . .

The lead-in words may also suggest effort or intention with respect to the infinitive action:

try to scrape . . .
ready to applaud . . .

They sometimes indicate control (or absence of control) over the action by those who perform it:

we . . . shall presently be forced to clear up . . .
we shall not be able to produce . . .

Or they may link speakers and words: "is said to carry . . ." There are many other possibilities; as it happens, all of these examples are from one page of the preface to "The Apple Cart" (StJ, 176). On this page, only one infinitive does *not* establish a relationship between action and mind: "thirty years . . . to do thirty minutes work." Given Shaw's emphasis on mind-event infinitives, it seems fair to place the infinitive in the same camp with other devices of Shaw's personal style.

This cluster of habits stretches into still other stylistic compartments that are somewhat surprising, into abstract diction, for instance. What is unexpected is to find Shaw relying on abstract diction to the same extent that other writers do. For one thing, his own occasional remarks show a distrust of abstractions as intellectual tools. In the beginning of *Everybody's Political What's What?* he describes the illusory feeling of ideological unity that politicians create by staying in "the region of abstraction." This unity is valuable in wartime, but for a program of real social improvement the abstract phrases are "as useless . . . as algebraic symbols which represent quantities but give no information as to quantities of what" (p. 5). And, in an entirely different context, he makes a plea for abandoning the "perfectly idle" abstract descriptions of people that make every obituary sound alike; the underlying words and deeds are what count. Once in a while he actually deflates a set of abstractions by translating them into less glamorous equivalents:

University professors elaborating the process known as the education of a gentleman . . .; workmen doing their work as badly and slowly as they dare . . .; employers starving and overworking their hands . . .: these are the actual living material of those imposing abstractions known as the State, the Church, the Law, the Constitution, Education, the Fine Arts, and Industry. (Essays, 101)

On the whole Shaw does obey his own proscription in so far as it is a proscription against vagueness and pomposity. As I have been arguing in this chapter, his thought is always animated by a vivid awareness of specific people in specific predicaments. Bentley puts it well:

In the realm of the general and the abstract Shaw is always gravitating towards the particular and the concrete. The peculiar intensity with which he sees human beings and the peculiar intensity with which he feels life as he lives it—these things are at the bottom of his politics and his philosophy.[17]

Yet Shaw does use many abstractions. A count of abstract nouns (using one accepted definition of abstract: not having a material thing as referent) shows him relying on them fairly heavily, in spite of his equally heavy weighting of names and personal pronouns.[18]

The explanation is close at hand. Concrete nouns ("kitten" and "cigar") most often refer to neatly bordered masses and to sets of these isolated bits. They take the world as it is most

obviously *given* to us in the *Gestalten* of perception. Abstract
nouns, on the other hand, play fast and loose with such vision-
bound categories. They represent a conceptual arrangement of
experience along other lines, sometimes more esoteric visual,
auditory, and tactile lines ("sound," "circularity," "roughness"),
but usually along lines much farther removed from immediate
experience, as with "justice," "romance," "opinion," and so on.
Such terms bespeak a highly intricate cross-sectioning of experience. They are the product, in short, of *mind*. Abstract words
enter a language relatively late, in any significant number:
most of ours in English are clearly derivative from adjectives
("wholeness") or verbs ("knowledge"). It is natural that they
should abound in the work of an apostle of intellect like Shaw.

And there is another equally compelling correlation between his use of abstractions and his attitude toward man's role
in the world. Since the play of thought and of emotion does not
yield (except in neurology and in metaphor) to description in
concrete terms, the language of mental activity is necessarily
the language of abstraction; "mind," "thought," "feeling," "understanding," and "confusion" have no concrete equivalents.

To see what role such abstract nouns play in Shaw's diction,
it is only necessary to scan a section of his prose and set the
mental abstractions against the others:

MENTAL	OTHERS
conversion	tradition
dismay	commission [?]
proposal	result
joy	business
genius	side
fecundity [mental]	time

performance	classic
impertinences	play [?]
feeling	life [?]
reputation	case
career	
truth	
care	
potboiler [?]	

(HH, 131—question marks indicate uncertainty as to classification)

Not only do the mental abstractions account for the majority of the total, but they are by far the more obtrusive. "Case," "side," "time," and "result" are words that one passes over without much attention, so commonplace are they. And note that three of the words in the right-hand column—"commission," "business," and "life"—have to do with people, if not with mental action.

Shaw's tendency is to give abstractions a prominence in his prose to match the significance he attaches to mind in natural process. When he makes "Darwinism" or a surrogate pronoun the grammatical subject in seven successive sentences (the verbs it governs being active and transitive with one exception), he suggests that ideas have consequences (Back, lx–lxi). And when he sets Lamarckianism against its successor, a vital contrast for him, he calls it the way of "life, will, aspiration, and achievement," and Darwinism the way of "hunger, death, stupidity, delusion, chance, and bare survival" (Back, xliii). Abstractions of mind and soul clearly dominate the positive side. Such words bring experience under the aspect of mind, both through their peculiar independent and rational organization of sense data and through their essential role in talk about thinking and feeling. For these reasons it is not surprising to find Shaw stressing abstraction, in spite of his genuine protests against its oratorical misuse.

Another superficially surprising Shavianism is the high proportion of adjectives.[19] It has been fashionable for some time to suggest that good writing is spare writing, and that in the effort to strip down his prose the good writer shuns adjectives as effete and inessential ornament. Yet the adjective is an instrument of precision, as any word must be if the user is competent, for it serves to tighten up categories. The words "red, red rose" or "outrageous fortune" cover a narrower semantic space than the words "rose" or "fortune" alone.

But to clear adjectives of the charge of inefficiency is not to explain their numbers in Shaw's prose. I think he favors them partly because, like abstract nouns, they are a vehicle for expressing mental concepts and personal qualities. In the junctions (combinations of "head" and modifier) where most of them reside they often give character to a person or group of people (all examples are from p. 51 of *The Doctor's Dilemma*):

sympathetic readers
medical profession [twice]
ignorant, shallow, credulous, half-miseducated, pecuniarily anxious
    people
advertizing druggist
humane persons
student-led mobs
British public
poor Peculiars

In addition, two of the three adjectives *not* in junctions ("surprised" and "afraid") modify personal nouns as predicate adjectives. Still other adjectives modify abstractions of mental state: "faintest conception," "virtuous indignation," "so creditable and salutary a sentiment," "vulgar lay capacity," and "indispensable" passion of cruelty.

It may have been noticed that both these groups contain some adjectives with evaluative as well as descriptive weight. "Ignorant" and the others in the long series, "humane," "virtuous," "creditable and salutary," and "indispensable" all praise or condemn in addition to adding information. The moral impulse is uniquely human; and evaluation is a characteristically mental activity, a fact suggested by the words social scientists often use to describe it, "judgment" and "attitude." Evaluation is also a characteristically Shavian activity. The categories "good" and "bad" are among those to which he seeks rigid boundaries (see Chapter I), partly, no doubt, because they involve the processing of facts by mind, the application of emotions to things. Thus the fact that adjectives frequently carry evaluative meaning is another point in their favor for Shaw. In addition to those listed above there are on the same page two others almost exclusively attitudinal, "noble" profession, and "real" remedy (in the sense of "best and only genuine" remedy). When these three groups of adjectives, all having to do with people or mind, are subtracted from the total number on this page, only one remains, the physically descriptive "heavy." For the most part Shaw's adjectives either describe people and mental action or place observed things under the aegis of the author's mind.

Add to the adjectives of attitude, character, and mind the abstractions that deal with mentality, plus a few concrete nouns, verbs, and adverbs of the same category, and the total is quite striking. At the risk of running my point into the ground I want to insert one last catalogue to support it. The following are words of this rather loosely defined class appearing on a page of the preface to "John Bull's Other Island" (21):

Adjectives:

humorous	witty	wilful
romantic	ridiculous	patriotic
gay	lazy	admiring
sceptical	affectionate	religious
wrong [twice]	educated	revolutionary
vital	intellectual [twice]	right
amusing	impressed	sentimental
blaspheming	faithless	shabby-genteel

Abstractions:

blackguardism	fatheadedness	distinction [mental]
sentiment	mind	laziness
faithlessness	infatuations	slovenliness
worthlessness [twice]	wit	belief
impotence	humor	stupidity [twice]
conclusion	idiosyncrasies	trustworthiness
wrong-headedness	wilfulness	vice
vivacity	efficiency	question
instability	truth	danger
error	love	dissoluteness
genius	doubt	chivalry

Verbs:

appreciating	grasps	confused
mistaking	contended	mistrusts
conclude	duped	seem

Adverbs:

intellectually [twice]	severely	dangerously

Concrete Nouns:

zealots	wits [wags]

On pages such as this, and there are many, the bulk of the vocabulary (other than function words) has to do with attitudes, thought, character, or values. In this way Shaw's lexicon jibes with his *Weltanschauung*. He intrudes mind into his style as his evolutionary theory intrudes mind into the universe.

4. THE PASSIONATE INTELLECT

Philosophy, according to Bertrand Russell, "springs from a kind of self-assertion: a belief that our purposes have an important relation to the purposes of the universe."[20] As such, he says, it is a mentally immature activity, for mature thought would seek truth whatever the emotional consequences, while philosophy has usually had ulterior motives. Shaw, like Russell, campaigns against philosophical wishful thinking, notably in his Ibsenite rejection of sentimental ideals. Hard fact is always shattering society's house of beliefs because that house is made of mirrors that give the residents a familiar and reassuring picture of the universe, but hide the outside world and its throwers of rocks. The nineteenth century has offered a series of stern lessons on "the folly of believing anything for no better reason than that it is pleasant to believe it" (Essays, 28).

Yet Shaw's own inadequacy as a philosopher results partly from his deep emotional involvement in ideas. I have remarked on the language in which Shaw deplores Darwinism—its "hideous fatalism" that makes the heart sink into a heap of sand, and its "damnable" reduction of beauty and mind to blind accident (Back, xlii). This is the language of passion, not the language of the detached philosopher. A system built to satisfy such a powerful moral drive as this is not on the face of it likely to survive rigorous criticism. And some of Shaw's remarks on socialism

suggest that the same deep urge to find man in control of external forces impels his social thinking too. Thus he claims that
it is "impossible to express the relief with which we discover
that our hearts were all along right" about the corruption of the
social order; "It was terrible to feel this, and yet to fear that it
could not be helped—that the poor must starve and make you
ashamed of your dinner—that they must shiver and make you
ashamed of your warm overcoat" (Essays, 30). Shaw feels "in-
debted" to economics for showing men the way to make an end
of such slavery, and his socialism is surely animated more by
humane compassion for the poor and humanistic disgust with
capitalism's subterfuge and venality than by purely intellectual
delight in having an adequate description and explanation of
economic phenomena.

Whether an idea is philosophical or social, Shaw has little
purely esthetic interest in it. It must measure up to the crucial
test of applicability to human conduct: If we accept this idea,
what effect will it have on society? What will it do to our stature
as men? Is it defeatist? These are the questions Shaw asks himself, and they all reduce to one question: Will the idea help man
impose his will on his surroundings? With such a simple criterion
for truth, Shaw has great confidence in his ability to evaluate
ideas. The higher man depends less on systematic thought and
more on instinct, for evolution is always reducing slow and difficult thought processes to effortless second nature. Thus Shaw
hopes that "the most prolonged and difficult operations of our
minds may yet become instantaneous, or, as we call it, instinctive" (Back, xxvii). And even in the primitive twentieth century
a thinker who is tuned in to the Life Force may have almost perfect pitch in sounding out ideas: he may judge them by their
emotional rightness.

This is not to say that Shaw is intellectually lazy. Nothing could be farther from the truth. The passion with which he accepts or rejects ideas is the passion of the intellect (he habitually classifies intellect among the passions), no easy taskmaster for a thinker. Still, Shaw defines a passion as "an overwhelming impulse towards a more abundant life" (Delusions, 319)—and no passion other than the passion for truth is likely to serve a philosopher well. But the truth may turn out to lead to a *less* abundant life, unhappily. Shaw permits philosophy to serve his humanistic optimism, and the result is a resonant affirmation of faith in man and mind rather than a cogent system. Let me suggest a permutation of my chapter title: Shaw is a *philosophical socialist,* in that his social thought springs from ideological rather than factual roots; and he is a *social philosopher,* in that his philosophy follows the grail of human betterment. In his thought, as in his style, a concern with that which is peculiarly human is the driving force.

In a sense, my exploratory tour of Shaw's style and thought has moved, by four different trails, to the same end: an affirmation of human mind and order, as against the destructive forces of mechanism and chance. The quest for likenesses is a struggle to overcome, through the organizing energies of mind, the threatening randomness of experience. In embracing discontinuity, on the other hand, Shaw rejects the mechanical tyranny of past over present and asserts man's right to *control* himself and his world, rather than doing (or thinking, or writing) what was done (or thought, or written) last time. Similarly, his affection for the everlasting "nay" represents an unalterable opposition to the blockhead, the man who impoverishes human life by his slavery to "ideals" and deceptions. And of course the pertinence of this last chapter to the theme of cerebral control needs no comment. The simplification I am making is perhaps itself Shavian in extent, but it is what the evidence of this study seems to demand. If the dazzling complexity of Shaw's work can be reduced, only for a moment, to manageable, namable proportions, then "apostle of mind" is what Shaw must be called.

NOTES

Notes

NOTES TO THE INTRODUCTION

1. *Style in Prose Fiction; English Institute Essays*, 1958, ed. Harold C. Martin (New York, 1959). My essay, "Prolegomena to the Analysis of Prose Style," occupies pages 1–24 of that volume.

2. Noam Chomsky has set the theoretical course for grammarians in his *Syntactic Structures* (The Hague, 1957), where he sketched the type of grammatical system that will be necessary. When Chomsky's work is digested by linguists (he himself is working on English grammar), and when more of them have turned to the extraordinarily difficult task of describing English structure, we may begin to learn, not only about nouns and adjectives, but about the infinitely more subtle distinctions that any speaker must have subconsciously mastered, and that tantalize every student of language.

NOTES TO CHAPTER I

1. "Two Aspects of Language and Two Types of Aphasic Disturbances," in Jakobson and Morris Halle, *Fundamentals of Language* (The Hague, 1956).

2. This distinction parallels Saussure's famous one between *rapports syntagmatiques* and *rapports associatifs* in: Ferdinand de Saussure, *Cours de Linguistique Générale* (Paris, 1955), pp. 170–75. Saussure, however, restricts associative links by equating them with semantic connections in the mind: roughly, *connotations*. I prefer Jakobson's notion of similarity, since it includes purely grammatical likenesses as well.

3. The pace of Shaw's style has been singled out for praise by Dixon Scott in "The Innocence of George Bernard Shaw," in *Men of Letters* (London, 1916), pp. 19–23.

4. My references to Shaw's works are, wherever possible, to the *Ayot St. Lawrence Edition of The Collected Works of Bernard Shaw* (New York, 1930–32). Page references apply also to *The Works of Bernard Shaw* (London, 1930–32), for which the same type was used. In the following key to my in-text references the volumes belong to The Ayot St. Lawrence edition unless otherwise specified.

And	*Androcles and the Lion, Overruled, Pygmalion*
Back	*Back to Methuselah*
Black Girl	*The Adventures of the Black Girl in Her Search for God* (London, 1932)
Delusions	*Doctors' Delusions, Crude Criminology, Sham Education*
Dilemma	*The Doctor's Dilemma, Getting Married, The Shewing-Up of Blanco Posnet*
EPWW	*Everybody's Political What's What?* (London, 1944)
Essays	*Essays in Fabian Socialism*
HH	*Heartbreak House, Great Catherine, Playlets of the War*
IK	*The Irrational Knot*
Imm	*Immaturity*
IWG	*The Intelligent Woman's Guide to Socialism and Capitalism*
IWG (Stan. Ed.)	*The Intelligent Woman's Guide to Socialism, Capitalism, Sovietism and Fascism,* Standard Edition (London, 1932)
JBOI	*John Bull's Other Island, How He Lied to Her Husband, Major Barbara*
M&S	*Man and Superman*
Mis	*Misalliance, The Dark Lady of the Sonnets, Fanny's First Play*

Music	*Music in London 1890–94* (3 vols.)
PP&R	*Pen Portraits and Reviews*
PPU	*Plays Pleasant and Unpleasant* (2 vols.)
QI	*The Quintessence of Ibsenism, The Perfect Wagnerite, The Sanity of Art*
Simp	*The Simpleton, The Six, and The Millionairess. Being Three More Plays by Bernard Shaw* (London, 1936)
SSS	*Sixteen Self Sketches, Standard Edition* (London, 1949)
StJ	*Saint Joan, The Apple Cart*
Terry	*Ellen Terry and Bernard Shaw: A Correspondence,* ed. Christopher St. John (London, 1931)
Theatres	*Our Theatres in the Nineties* (3 vols.)
3PP	*Three Plays for Puritans; The Devil's Disciple, Caesar and Cleopatra, Captain Brassbound's Conversion*
Too True	*Too True to Be Good, Village Wooing & On the Rocks. Three Plays by Bernard Shaw* (London, 1934)
War	*What I Really Wrote About the War*

5. See Appendix I, Table 1.

6. I mean this literally as a conjecture about the mental processes of the writer. There is no use pretending that style (or content) is prophylactically insulated from the mind of the writer. Of course action, ideas, and style all issue from a mentality, whatever the scruples of critical theory, and I propose to speculate from time to time about Shaw's mentality, though that is not the main purpose of my analysis.

7. Eric Bentley, *Bernard Shaw* (New York, 1957), p. 159.

8. P. 160.

9. Quoted in Pearson's *G. B. S., A Full Length Portrait* (New York, 1942), p. 196.

10. One of the tenets of Creative Evolution is that the experience of the past is condensed in the living, and this notion of a symbiotic mental relationship between man and his ancestors is merely the in-

verse of Shaw's vision of history, which projects the experience of the living into the lives of the dead.

11. "Things" in the broadest sense, including events, concepts, situations, etc.

12. See Appendix I, Table 2.

13. He is also making a more direct comparison, for the preceding clause runs "I should not object to a law to compel everybody to read two newspapers . . ." There is no necessity for a conditional clause to be accompanied by such a foil as this, but it is surprising how often such pairs occur in Shaw.

14. See Appendix I, Table 3.

15. See Jerome Bruner, Jacqueline J. Goodnow, George A. Austin, A Study of Thinking (New York ,1956), pp. 2–3.

16. Bruner, pp. 3–5.

17. Pearson, p. 143.

18. Pearson, p. 359.

19. New York Times Book Review, Nov. 18, 1945. Quoted by Bentley, p. xix.

20. Archibald Henderson, George Bernard Shaw: Man of the Century (New York, 1956), pp. xxxi–xxxii.

21. In Bernard Shaw and the Nineteenth-Century Tradition (Norman, Oklahoma, 1958), Julian B. Kaye traces the opposition of intelligence and laissez-faire mechanism to Carlyle (pp. 10–11), who was one of Shaw's spiritual mentors. Kaye's book usefully points to many nineteenth-century antecedents of Shaw's thought, but I would resist the conclusion that such genealogy goes far toward explaining Shaw. The ideas were there for him to build on, well and good. The question still remains what there was in Shaw that made him adopt precisely these ideas out of the infinity that were available to him.

22. Mechanism antagonizes Shaw wherever he encounters it. He finds the humor mechanistic in "The Importance of Being Earnest," and sums up his reservations about the play by calling it a "mechanical rabbit" (quoted by Pearson, p. 147).

23. George S. Klein, "The Personal World Through Perception,"

in *Perception; an Approach to Personality*, eds. Robert R. Blake and Glenn V. Ramsey (New York, 1951), pp. 328–55.

24. See Else Frenkel-Brunswik, "Intolerance of Ambiguity as an Emotional and Perceptual Personality Variable," in *Perception and Personality; a Symposium*, eds. Jerome S. Bruner and David Krech (Durham, North Carolina, 1950), p. 133. Frenkel-Brunswik takes the terms from K. Goldstein and M. Scheerer, *Abstract and Concrete Behavior, Psychological Monographs*, 1941, vol. 53, no. 239.

25. Blake and Ramsey, p. 335.

26. George S. Klein and Herbert Schlesinger, "Where is the Perceiver in Perceptual Theory?" in *Perception and Personality*, pp. 37–38.

27. Bruner and Krech, pp. 108–43. Frenkel-Brunswik does not use the terms "leveler" and "sharpener," but her categories are quite similar.

28. P. 140. There is little point in classifying Shaw with Frenkel Brunswik's prejudiced children, but it may be worth noting that as a boy he was a considerable snob. He was so humiliated at having been sent briefly to a school where the other students were Catholics and sons of tradesmen that he kept the fact secret for over eighty years (SSS, 42–43).

29. Victor Erlich, "Gogol and Kafka: A Note on Realism and Surrealism," in *For Roman Jakobson*, ed. Morris Halle (The Hague, 1956), p. 101.

30. *The Star*. Sept. 27, 1930; quoted by Henderson, p. 203.

31. Quoted by Henderson, p. 211.

32. There are a very few such clichés that pick their point of reference from the bottom of the relevant scale ("clear as mud," for instance), but their purpose is ironic.

33. See Fries, *The Structure of English*, p. 89.

34. See Appendix I, Table 4.

35. Fries, pp. 92–94.

36. See Appendix I, Table 5.

37. See Appendix I, Table 6.

NOTES TO CHAPTER II

1. I do not mean to be talking metaphysics or social theory here; I am merely trying to establish a view of historical change that is congenial to common sense and the ordinary human way of viewing things.

2. That Shaw is quick to find likenesses between men and situations separated by centuries (see Chapter I) is irrelevant to my present contention: with his penchant for similarity he sees the laws of behavior and historical causation as the same in all ages, but is nonetheless willing both to have society altered and to grant that change has taken place. It is a "superstition," he sometimes says, "that human nature cannot be changed." (Essays, 310).

3. Quoted by Pearson in G.B.S., A Full Length Portrait, p. 169.

4. Quoted by Archibald Henderson in George Bernard Shaw: Man of the Century, p. 50.

5. Pearson, p. 170, and others. Shaw himself took the play lightly.

6. Compare Shaw's famous letters, which take much of their sparkle from his willingness to contradict, even to astound, his correspondents.

7. Quoted by Henderson, p. 46.

8. William Irvine, The Universe of G. B. S. (New York, 1949), p. 122.

9. Quoted by Henderson, p. 727, from The New York Times, January 6, 1929.

10. Quoted by Henderson, p. 196, from "Who I Am, and What I Think," Part II, The Candid Friend, May 18, 1901. The essay appears slightly revised in Sixteen Self Sketches.

11. Appositions also follow from his favoring of similarity order, and Shaw's moderately heavy use of them is relevant to the findings of Chapter I as well. See Appendix I, Table 7.

12. Bonamy Dobree, Modern Prose Style (Oxford, 1934), pp. 12–13.

13. I do not impugn Shaw's clarity or suggest that he became

diffuse. His writing remains incisive and crammed with facts until the end.

14. An "Intermezzo" after Chapter XXXVI declares him to be finished with "facts" and ready to go on to metaphysics. Chapter XL, "For the Reviewers," says: "The pressing need for breaking off this unfinishable book has now become imperative." Its last chapter begins: "This book can never be finished any more than the Annual Register can. But each of its successive writers must stop somewhere, not always because they have no more to say . . . but because they are tired of saying it . . . I must stop, leaving much unsaid." And the book ends: "As to the future, beginning with the year 1944— *(to be continued by them that can)."*

15. Quoted by Henderson, p. 387.

16. *Bernard Shaw and Mrs. Patrick Campbell: Their Correspondence*, ed. Alan Dent (London, 1952), p. 83.

17. Victor Erlich, *Russian Formalism; History—Doctrine* (The Hague, 1955), p. 150.

18. See Claude E. Shannon and Warren Weaver, *The Mathematical Theory of Communication* (Urbana, Ill., 1949). Most of my information comes from Weaver's article at the end of this book.

19. Shannon and Weaver, p. 100.

20. The redundancy of English is about 50 per cent using *letters* as the unit (Shannon and Weaver, p. 104). If *phonemes* are taken as the unit, the redundancy is about 99.9 per cent (H. A. Gleason, Jr., *An Introduction to Descriptive Linguistics*, New York, 1955, p. 282). I know of no comparable figure using *words* as the unit, but would expect it to be somewhat below 50 per cent.

21. John Rupert Firth, *Papers in Linguistics* (Oxford, 1957), p. 32.

22. Technically (and appropriately) interference with communication is called "noise."

23. Another reason for the high entropy of his idiolect is the large size of his lexicon. When the digital computers get around to doing a Shaw concordance, they will show his vocabulary to be unusually broad.

NOTES TO CHAPTER III

1. "In the Days of My Youth," from *Mainly About People*, Sept. 17, 1898. Quoted by Henderson in *George Bernard Shaw: Man of the Century*, p. 16.

2. Quoted in Pearson's *G. B. S.; A Full Length Portrait*, p. 21.

3. "In the Days of My Youth," quoted by Henderson, p. 48.

4. Quoted by Henderson, p. 377.

5. Henderson, p. 740.

6. Bruner and Krech, *Perception and Personality*, p. 141.

7. Though I do not wish to press the point, there is more than a little paranoia in the running battles Shaw carries on in letters to the daily papers, where apparently he was subject to considerable abuse. And he does seem to take a special delight in relating the trials to which his superiority makes him subject. Of Mussolini's regime he says, "I, being a bit of a psychologist myself, also understood the situation, and was immediately denounced by the refugees and their champions as an anti-democrat, a hero-worshipper of tyrants, and all the rest of it" (Simp, 117).

8. It bears repeating that "The Revolutionist's Handbook" is written by Jack Tanner, who perhaps exceeds even Shaw in obstreperousness. But his rhetoric, like his revolutionism, differs from that of his creator in degree, not in kind.

9. See Appendix I, Table 8.

10. See Appendix I, Table 9.

11. Eric Bentley, *Bernard Shaw*, p. 72.

12. This point is developed in Chapters III and IV of Arthur H. Nethercot's *Men and Supermen; The Shavian Portrait Gallery* (Cambrige, Mass., 1954). The categories *realist* and *idealist* seem to me the most fruitful of all those that Nethercot applies to Shaw's characters.

NOTES TO CHAPTER IV

1. The difference can be more rigorously stated. For the best treatment, see Noam Chomsky, *Syntactic Structures* (The Hague, 1957), pp. 61–72.

2. See Appendix I, Table 10.

3. In spite of Shaw's youthful love affairs, it is on the whole true that his passions ran more to the intellect than to the flesh. A world without matter would have suited him well.

4. See Appendix I, Table 11.

5. See Appendix I, Table 12.

6. Robert B. Lees, *The Grammar of English Nominalizations*, Part II of the *International Journal of American Linguistics*, vol. 26, no. 3, July, 1960, 57–64.

7. See Appendix I, Table 13.

8. See Appendix I, Table 14.

9. Only from his plays, seemingly, does he bar his own specific experiences. "The Philanderer" renders bits of Shaw's London Life, but in general he does not put his friends or his experiences into drama.

10. See Appendix I, Table 15.

11. Quoted by Archibald Henderson in *George Bernard Shaw: Man of the Century*, p. 872.

12. See Appendix I, Table 16.

13. See Appendix I, Table 17.

14. Jean Piaget, *The Language and Thought of the Child*, tr. Marjorie Gabain (New York, 1955), pp. 203–4.

15. See Appendix I, Table 18.

16. See Appendix I, Table 19.

17. Eric Bentley, *Bernard Shaw*, xxiii.

18. See Appendix I, Table 20.

19. See Appendix I, Table 21.

20. Bertrand Russell, *Unpopular Essays* (New York, 1950), p. 57.

APPENDICES

Appendix I

I OFFER the following counts with no particular fanfare, in the hope only that they will supplement the evidence already presented. Since statistics generally lend an air of infallibility to the documents they adorn, it may be well for me to state briefly a few things that limit the usefulness of these particular statistics.

For one thing, not nearly all of my descriptive statements about Shaw's style are reducible to numbers; for the whole of Chapter II, for instance, I have been able to invoke almost no statistical support. Some stylistic features cannot be counted, and some occur too infrequently to appear in short, randomly chosen excerpts. So the twenty tables of this appendix constitute only fragmentary backing for my analyses.

In the second place, the samples I have used, 2600 words from Shaw and 2600 from each of five contemporaries, are not large enough to yield highly reliable conclusions for many of the counts. For instance the numbers of quotations and of questions (Tables 9 and 11) that occur in this space are too small to give much assurance that the ratios would hold if the sample were increased to, say, 100,000 words. Table 19 contains disconcerting proof of this fact.

In spite of these reservations I believe my statistics to be convincing, for this reason: throughout the twenty tables Shaw consistently runs ahead of the control group when I have so predicted, and though a greatly expanded sample would probably reduce or even eliminate his margin in some counts, it would just as surely increase his margin in others. Hence the set of tables as a whole gives reasonable proof that my critical reading of Shaw has been sound. Since this conclusion is the important one, I have allowed myself to shirk the job of compiling extremely large counts. In any case, 2600 words is easily a large enough sample to reveal the style of an author.

Another related danger is that of bias in choosing the samples, and there is no point in protesting my innocence in this matter, since if the statistics were rigged I would be unlikely to say as much, and since bias may in any case operate unconsciously. The answer, of course, would have been to pick excerpts completely at random, and I cannot claim to have done that. But the restrictions I did consciously impose were such as to bring the selections on all fours with one another, rather than to slant the results. That is, for the control group I sought passages that were roughly comparable in subject matter to those by Shaw, giving emphasis to social commentary, philosophy, and the like. To have taken instead passages of, say, narrative or description would have largely invalidated all comparisons— would, in fact, have led to much more striking contrasts between Shaw and the others than I have actually uncovered on many counts.

Finally, there is the difficulty of deciding what to count.

In the first place, few of my counts are neatly circumscribed by the boundaries of just one lexical or syntactic class. Grammatical classes do not correspond precisely to all the stylistic dimensions I wish to measure, and rather than have tight categories and meaningless statistics I chose to have hybrid categories and useful counts. It would seem, anyhow, that consistency in counting is the main thing, not the initial decision on what to count. But this brings me to a second difficulty: given loose classes like some of mine, and given the embryonic state of English descriptive grammar at present, there invariably arise questionable cases, on which the rules of selection do not unambiguously pronounce. Is "society" an abstract noun or not? Is "higher animals" an instance of a comparison? And so on. I can only hope that in making such decisions I have not allowed the wish for statistical confirmation of my hypothesis to overbalance scholarly detachment, and that I have been as consistent as possible in applying my criteria.

These are melancholy preliminaries; but on the assumption that the reader is still in attendance, let me proceed with a list of the samples used:

SHAW

The Intelligent Woman's Guide, pp. 102–5; the first five paragraphs of Chapter 26. 936 wds.

Back to Methuselah, pp. lxxix–lxxx; all of "What to Do With the Legends" and "A Lesson from Science to the Churches," and up to "Cabinet Ministers as well" in the next chapter. 623 wds.

The Quintessence of Ibsenism, pp. 131–33; "There can be no" to "promiscuous amours." 557 wds.

John Bull's Other Island, pp. 42–44; the chapter entitled "A Natural Right." 467 wds.

Total: 2583 wds.

THE CONTROL GROUP

W. B. Yeats, *Per Amica Silentia Lunae* (New York, 1918), pp. 44–58 and 61–65; sections X through XIII; sections I through III, and from the beginning of Chapter VI to "in the photographic camera." 2586 wds.

Bertrand Russell, *Mysticism and Logic* (Penguin Books, Harmondsworth, Middlesex, 1953), pp. 98–107; "We are thus left" to "business of philosophy." 2640 wds.

Sidney and Beatrice Webb, *Industrial Democracy* (London, 1920), pp. 590–97; "We can now form" to "schools of thought." 2560 wds.

G. K. Chesterton, *Orthodoxy* (New York, 1909), pp. 68–80; "But they cannot escape" to "from the top throughout." 2608 wds.

Oscar Wilde, *The Soul of Man Under Socialism and Other Essays*, *The Complete Works of Oscar Wilde*, Vol. X (New York, 1927), pp. 56–62; "It is to be noted" to "His perfection through pain," and *Intentions, Works*, Vol. V, pp. 117–22; "It is true" to "had no art critics." 2520 wds.

To give adequate representation to all Shaw's major works would have been impossible, given the limits of my endurance; so I chose only four excerpts from prose written during his prime and covering a variety of subjects: socialism, religion, ethics, political rights. In the control group, Yeats writes of the materialization of souls through the agency of a witch, Russell of science and philosophy, the Webbs of trade unionism, Chesterton of decadence in modern thought (that of Nietzsche especially), and Wilde of individualism, joy, and pain.

Here are the counts, with a few explanatory and interpretative remarks.

TABLE 1: *The long series.*

I counted every series, within a sentence, of four or more members. (Technically, these are constructions produced by

Noam Chomsky's rule for conjunction, *Syntactic Structures*, p. 36.)

	Number of series	Series per 1000 wds.
Chesterton	3	1.1
Wilde	4	1.6
Webbs	2	.8
Russell	0	.0
Yeats	1	.4
Av. of control group		.8
Shaw	7	2.7

	Total members	Members per 1000 wds.
Chesterton	12	4.6
Wilde	18	7.1
Webbs	11	4.3
Russell	0	.0
Yeats	4	1.5
Av. of control group		3.5
Shaw	44	17.0

TABLE 2: *Comparative forms, including the superlative.*

For the most part the text explains this category. I did not include "such_____as," which is only a form of cataloguing; and I also omitted "more or less," which does not involve comparison.

	Number of comparisons	Comparisons per 1000 wds.
Chesterton	27	10.3
Wilde	12	4.8
Webbs	23	9.0
Russell	23	8.6
Yeats	20	7.7
Av. of control group		8.1
Shaw	44	17.1

TABLE 3: *"Would."*

This count does not include the past tense, "would have," and includes "should" only when it is clearly hypothetical rather than ethical. Obviously a larger sample is necessary before such a count becomes fully trustworthy, but Shaw's leadership in this usage is so great here as to be interesting, in spite of the small absolute numbers involved.

	Occurrences of "would"	Occurrences per 1000 wds.
Chesterton	3	1.1
Wilde	1	.4
Webbs	5	2.0
Russell	10	3.8
Yeats	3	1.2
Av. of control group		1.7
Shaw	14	5.4

TABLE 4: *All-or-nothing determiners.*

As in the text, I counted nominative uses of these words, as well as derivatives such as "nobody" and "whoever." I also included "only" in such usages as "the only____s," which clearly have the semantic function of specifying a complete class. It is not particularly surprising, I think, to find Chesterton ranking so high on this count, since he, like Shaw, seeks extremities and violent forms of expression.

	Total number of all-or-nothing determiners	Number per 1000 wds.
Chesterton	50	19.2
Wilde	29	11.4
Webbs	31	12.1
Russell	30	11.4
Yeats	30	11.6
Av. of control group		13.2
Shaw	43	16.7

TABLE 5: *Degree words.*

Russell is the sport here. A glance at his degree words shows that they are not generally intensifiers, however, but the very opposite. His prose is full of thoughtful, qualifying, hesitating degree words such as "fundamentally," "essentially," and "more or less" (which locution occurs three times in this sample). When he uses "most" it is in locutions like "one of the most_____," which soften the intensifying force of the degree word. That a high score in such a count can mean extravagance for Shaw and caution for Russell is unfortunate but true, and goes to show once again that statistics cannot at present be the final refuge of stylistic criticism. In any case, it is only the large number of degree words used by Russell that brings the total for the control group near the total for Shaw.

	No. of degree words	Degree wds. per 1000
Chesterton	11	4.2
Wilde	21	8.3
Webbs	27	10.6
Russell	42	15.9
Yeats	16	6.2
Av. of control group		9.1
Shaw	31	12.0

TABLE 6: *Degree intensity, extent, limits, quantity.*

Included here are words and constructions from several formal categories: 1) What are sometimes technically called "comparatives"—that is, adjectives modified by "-er," "more," "less," or "as," with syntactically dependent complements beginning with "than" or "as." (For a treatment of these complicated forms based on the principles of transformational grammar, see Carlota S. Smith, "A Class of Complex Modifiers in English," *Language,* XXXVII [1961], 342–365.) These forms either grade two adjectives as to intensity or grade two nouns according to the pertinence of one adjective to both ("a man more witty than wise," as against "a man more witty than the toastmaster"). 2) A closely related group of constructions which subordinate one sentence to another ("so____that____," "too____to____," and "____enough to____"; see Smith, pp. 360–361). 3) Degree words. 4) Superlatives. 5) Numbers. In addition, this table includes what I have called "all-or-nothing determiners" and some other words or locutions that are related to intensity etc. by meaning alone. That the count incorporates this semantically defined periphery detracts somewhat from its reliability, but I believe that the results are still interesting, especially in view of the large number of words and constructions involved.

	Number of words indicating limits, degree, etc.	Number per 1000 wds.
Chesterton	120	46
Wilde	80	32
Webbs	129	50
Russell	129	49
Yeats	102	39
Av. of control group		43
Shaw	165	64

TABLE 7: *Appositional structures.*

	Number of appositions	Appositions per 1000 wds.
Chesterton	7	2.7
Wilde	3	1.2
Webbs	2	.8
Russell	8	3.0
Yeats	8	3.1
Av. of control group		2.2
Shaw	11	4.3

TABLE 8: *Negatives.*

Again Chesterton spoils the picture, and again the reason is probably a genuine similarity in outlook between him and Shaw. Like Shaw, he is an exposer of fallacies, critic of the world around him, and drawer of distinctions. It would be interesting to count just the number of times Shaw or Chesterton denies an assertion made by the other.

	Negatives	Negatives per 1000 wds.
Chesterton	50	19.1
Wilde	40	15.9
Webbs	28	10.9
Russell	29	11.0
Yeats	30	11.6
Av. of control group		13.7
Shaw	53	20.6

TABLE 9: *Direction shifts.*

The numbers here are too small to be significant, but I include the count for its casual interest. Short though the sample from Russell is, his prominence in this count makes sense, for he procceds in his arguments by stating his opponent's case and then refuting it, a method characteristic of British philosophy in general.

	Number of shifts	Shifts per 1000 wds.
Chesterton	5	1.9
Wilde	2	.8
Webbs	1	.4
Russell	7	2.7
Yeats	0	.0
Av. of control group		1.2
Shaw	12	4.7

TABLE 10: *Request Utterances.*

The count includes independent clauses as well as complete sentences.

	Request utterances	Request utterances per 1000 wds.
Chesterton	3	1.1
Wilde	1	.4
Webbs	0	.0
Russell	2	.8
Yeats	6	2.3
Av. of control group		1.0
Shaw	15	5.8

TABLE 11: *Dependent Clauses.*

I counted gerundial phrases if they had direct objects. The relatively small difference between Shaw and the other writers is probably meaningful in view of the large numbers involved.

	Dependent clauses	Dependent clauses per 1000 wds.
Chesterton	124	47
Wilde	104	41
Webbs	98	38
Russell	129	49
Yeats	141	55
Av. of control group		46
Shaw	137	53

TABLE 12: *Quotations.*

I use the word "quotations" to include reports of actual or hypothetical speech not actually set in quotation marks. But I do not include any "indirect" quotations, as they are covered by Table 12. Nor do I include allusions, or quotations not attributed to a speaker. Again, a much larger sample is necessary, but this one may be suggestive.

	Quotations	Quotations per 1000 wds.
Chesterton	3	1.1
Wilde	1	.4
Webbs	0	.0
Russell	2	.8
Yeats	10	3.9
Av. of control group		1.2
Shaw	8	3.1

TABLE 13: *The introductory "that."*

The list in the text is a good indication of what I included in this count. I omitted occurrences of "so that" ("in order that") and "now that"; and of course I omitted all demonstratives and relatives.

	Introductory "that's"	"That's" per 1000 wds.
Chesterton	25	9.6
Wilde	10	4.0
Webbs	23	9.0
Russell	22	8.3
Yeats	14	5.4
Av. of control group		7.3
Shaw	41	15.9

TABLE 14: *References to beliefs, statements, propositions.*

This is another catchall category, whose boundaries are fuzzy, and this fact must dilute somewhat the impressiveness of the results. Yet the count is nonetheless striking (as in Table 13), and I should perhaps insist here on its appropriateness to my interpretation of Shaw, since not all of the evidence for the contentions of Chapter IV is so clear cut. The figures are the more impressive in that they do not subsume the counts of the preceding two tables. The reason for Russell's prominence here is, of course, that he, as a philosopher, is explicitly talking about propositions much of the time, rather than about Ireland, Ibsen, economics, and the like.

	References to propositions	References to propositions per 1000 wds.
Chesterton	93	35
Wilde	58	23
Webbs	93	36
Russell	105	40
Yeats	66	26
Av. of control group		32
Shaw	117	45

TABLE 15: *Proper names.*

I counted adjectival names such as "Irish," but omitted such capitalized nouns as "Church'" and "Papacy," and Shaw's Grand Abstractions—"Socialism" and other isms, which he tends to capitalize. I also excluded "Socialist," "Communist," and the like. A glance through the pages of *Orthodoxy* suggests that Chesterton does not normally use so many proper names as in this excerpt but that he does share Shaw's affection for personalized examples. Rather than say "a man," he will name a particular man or make up a hypothetical man named Jones.

	Proper names	Proper names per 1000 wds.
Chesterton	69	26
Wilde	43	17.1
Webbs	14	5.5
Russell	12	4.5
Yeats	32	12.4
Av. of control group		13.1
Shaw	74	29

TABLE 16: *Personal pronouns and words for which they can stand.*

The category is not so clearly defined as it may sound. "They," for instance, can refer either to people or to non-human entities. And nouns such as "Church" and "government" are troublesome. But more often than not the decisions are easy, so the count is not altogether arbitrary. It includes only words in a nominal position and omits the relative pronoun "who."

	Personal pronouns, etc.	Personal pronouns per 1000 wds.
Chesterton	264	101
Wilde	209	83
Webbs	149	58
Russell	84	32
Yeats	187	72
Av. of control group		69
Shaw	274	104

TABLE 17: *Proportion of grammatical subjects that are person words.*

Here I included the relative pronoun "who" and counted gerundial phrases if they had "subjects." The pre-eminence of Chesterton is accountable partly to a similarity in outlook to Shaw, partly to the somewhat special content of this excerpt.

	Number of person words as subjects	Other subjects	Percentage of person words in total
Chesterton	178	114	61
Wilde	120	130	48
Webbs	56	98	36
Russell	47	176	21
Yeats	126	114	52
Av. of control group			45
Shaw	128	96	57

TABLE 18: *Mental causation.*

This is another inexact category, and I made the count more by feel than by rule. On the whole, I included any causal nexus that had to do with motivation, thought, or personal action.

	Causal nexuses involving motivation	Motivational nexuses per 1000 wds.
Chesterton	23	8.7
Wilde	13	5.2
Webbs	15	5.9
Russell	10	3.8
Yeats	21	8.1
Av. of control group		6.4
Shaw	24	9.3

TABLE 19: *Infinitives.*

The count includes only those infinitives preceded by "to."

	Infinitives	Infinitives per 1000 wds.
Chesterton	32	12.3
Wilde	25	9.9
Webbs	31	12.1
Russell	34	12.9
Yeats	21	8.1
Av. of control group		11.1
Shaw	18	7.0

I could interpret these statistics as showing either that my sample was atypical or that my hypothesis was wrong. Understandably, I preferred the first interpretation; I therefore counted the infinitives in a new sample of Shaw's prose, twice as long as the original passage and taken from the same works (specifically, I used the sections immediately preceding and following the original samples).

In this sample Shaw averaged 15.3 infinitives per 1000 words, more than any member of the control group. Yet saving the count in this way is, of course, a Pyrrhic victory, since it calls all my other counts into question. I have reversed the verdict of my original tally here; why not elsewhere, and in an unfavorable direction? I can answer only that my counts are as likely to err against me as in my favor, and that the reliability of the statistics as a group is much higher than the reliability of any single table. It would be surprising indeed if a set of much larger counts upset the whole impact of these tables.

TABLE 20: *Abstract nouns.*

I counted gerunds with an article or determiner. There are some problems in a count such as this. A noun like "society" seems to have both abstract and concrete components, for one thing. For another, Yeats uses nouns such as "ghost" and "spirit," which are of dubious reference. And when a word that is normally concrete appears figuratively in an abstract sense, which way should it be counted? In spite of these difficulties the count is fairly reliable, since consistency is at least possible from one decision to the next.

As for the results, I expected they would place Shaw about in the middle, whereas actually they place him somewhat below center. They support my hypothesis only in that one might have expected a writer who uses a great many person words to use very few abstractions. In Shaw's case, talk of people does not *exclude* talk of abstractions, for the reasons presented in the text. It might be added, too, that both Russell and the Webbs are, to appearances, unusually abstract writers.

	Abstractions	Abstractions per 1000 wds.
Chesterton	302	116
Wilde	258	102
Webbs	471	184
Russell	471	179
Yeats	341	132
Av. of control group		143
Shaw	311	121

TABLE 21: *Adjectives.*

Here I include everything in Fries' Class 3, or in Sledd's positional class of "adjectivals" (*A Short Introduction to English Grammar*, pp. 92–94). The results are unspectacular enough, but as with Table 20, the purpose of the count is mainly to dispose of a false assumption—that Shaw, as a lucid and muscular writer, must eschew the adjective.

	Adjectives	Adjectives per 1000 wds.
Chesterton	175	64
Wilde	239	95
Webbs	280	109
Russell	226	86
Yeats	185	62
Av. of control group		85
Shaw	216	84

In my opinion, at least ten of these tables offer fairly impressive support for my case; they are numbers 1, 2, 3, 6, 8, 10, 13, 14, 15, and 16. Of the others, most are at least mildly convincing, and only one is a disaster. Let me repeat: I shall be satisfied if these statistics merely convince the reader that my description of Shaw's style is on the whole valid.

But it may be interesting to look for a moment at the particular comparisons offered in this appendix. My intuition about the writers used as controls was that stylistically Yeats and Russell differ a great deal from Shaw, that Wilde and the Webbs are closer, and that Chesterton is closer still. Chesterton's stylistic profile, as sketched by the counts, is indeed most like Shaw's. Some distance away come Russell, Yeats, and the Webbs, and Wilde is the most different. But be it remembered that I chose this set of tallies to measure crucial dimensions in *Shaw's* style, and that there is no reason to expect my counts to distinguish other writers from one another. A different set altogether would be necessary to establish the truly enormous differences between, say, Yeats and the Webbs.

Within the domain of these twenty-one counts, *all* the other writers are more like one another than any of them is like Shaw—which fact suggests that a small but carefully selected group of counts is more useful in isolating the style of a writer than would be a much larger but randomly chosen group. The evidence at hand is much too scanty to permit a confident generalization about style, but the generalization very tentatively indicated is that a writer's characteristic style is largely the product of relatively few idiosyncratic variations from the norm, out of the vast number possible. This hypothesis makes sense if style does reflect epistemic choice, for no writer, surely, differs from the rest in his entire epistemic alignment. Even a great eccentric is likely to share in large part the conceptual scheme, and hence the style, of his fellows.

Appendix II

TYPICALLY, critics study revisions to gain insight into the artistic process or the writer's meaning, or to follow the drift of his sensibility, the evolution of his technique. These inquiries often bear fruit when applied to poetry, for they rest on the justifiable assumption that a poet restlessly pushes toward perfection of form and of content—the best thoughts in the best words, as it were—and that something is to be learned from an examination of his efforts. Similarly, large-scale revisions of novels or of discursive works are perhaps best understood in terms of the structure and technique of the whole piece. But this approach is much more questionable when focused upon small stylistic revisions of expository prose. To be sure, the writer changes this or that phrase because he is trying to improve his book. Still, my limited experience with such revisions suggests that it is often impossible to discern in them consistent patterns of structural or tonal modification. When the manuscript has reached the stage of stylistic polishing, the writer has long since committed himself to a certain plan, a certain posture, a certain texture, and ceased tampering with the construction of the whole work. Instead he is concerned to perfect sentences or phrases, and his vision no longer extends beyond such an ambit. He seeks excellence, of course; but what is the most economical way to explain his means of achieving it?

Style, I have contended, is epistemic choice. One difficulty in applying the definition is that choice implies alternatives *rejected*, and in the finished product we cannot inspect those alternatives. Hence manuscript revisions offer a unique body of evidence for the confirmation or disconfirmation of my hypothesis. The writer strikes out one word and replaces it with another; or he simply deletes or adds a locution. If the manuscript survives, it offers the critic a look at both halves of an actual, historical decision.

A writer's style can generally be charted through the use of relatively few dimensions (see Appendix I), and it is reasonable to expect that his revisions will be distributed along those dimensions with unusual concentration. Put another way, some grammatical and semantic categories are particularly alive to the writer, since they have special relevance to his conceptual scheme, and he will continue to emphasize them in his late revisions, after others can no longer elicit his expressive energy.

With this notion in mind, I have examined the typescripts of Shaw's prose that reside in Houghton Library, Harvard. There are not many of these (Shaw did not like to preserve his working copy), but enough to provide an interesting sample of about five hundred short revisions. The significant typescripts in Houghton, and those to which I refer here, are as follows: 1) "A Degenerate's View of Nordau," as it appeared in Benjamin Tucker's paper, *Liberty*, July 27, 1895, and with Shaw's manuscript revisions for its ultimate publication as "The Sanity of

Art"; 2) the Preface to the second volume of *Plays Pleasant and Unpleasant;* 3) "The Select Committee on the Censorship"; and 4) "Rules for Play Producers." These I will abbreviate as follows: 1) SA, 2) PPU, 3) Cen, 4) Rules.

To begin with, let me concede that a good many of the revisions have little to do with Shavian idiosyncrasies of style. Shaw adds an adjective ("the ordinary *practical* comedy form," or "the *popular* demand"—PPU, 12), or substitutes "they did beat him" for "he was beaten" (PPU, 10), or changes "the production of" to "the composition of" (PPU, 12). Now even these changes impinge on categories that are important to Shaw's style—adjectives, person words, abstractions. But it would be almost impossible for any writer to revise without making alterations in these categories, so common are they. What is interesting is to note how often Shaw makes revisions within areas of peculiar relevance to his style.

By now these areas should be familiar enough to the reader, and I shall merely list a number of examples here, without comment. Words crossed out are those deleted by Shaw; words underlined are those added. Page numbers refer to the typescripts.

1. NEGATION
   a. *Deletions*
      to express . . . , ~~not to be a~~ . . . (SA, 3)
      in England, at least, ~~if not in Norway~~ (PPU, 1)
      as I ~~am no five-act blank verse playwright, but~~ have always . . . (PPU, 12)
      ~~There was nothing to prevent me from~~ . . . (PPU, 4)
      ~~This is not the opinion of~~ Nordau, ~~who~~ . . . ~~proceeds to~~ express(*es*) . . . (SA, 4)
   b. *Additions*
      Our managers will not dissent to this: the best of . . . (PPU, 16)

> *If there were no prosecution or no conviction, the local author-*
> *ity could not* . . . (Cen, 3) [follows a sentence that tells
> what would happen if there *were* a conviction]
> they *are not pattern designers; they* do not . . . (SA, 3)
> the difference between Caliban and Prospero is *not* that Pros-
> pero *has* . . . , *but that Prospero is* . . . (SA, 4)
> until then, *not being myself an inventor,* I must . . . (SA, 4)

c. *Changes*

> which was not dramatic music nor . . .
> which was neither dramatic music nor . . . (SA, 3)
>> instead of accepting it as . . .
>> could no longer accept it as . . . (SA, 2)
> is the rarest thing in nature . . .
> docs not exist in nature . . . (SA, 7)
> all managers are to some extent dependent
> no manager is wholly independent (PPU, 21)
>> easier of access
>> no harder of access (PPU, 16)
> I think this an excellent doctrine
> I am not afraid of this doctrine (SA, 4)
>> Liszt was no more . . .
>> Liszt tried hard to . . . (SA,3)
> the Home Secretary does not want
> no existing department wants (Cen, 1)
>> they do not want
>> they neither want nor understand (PPU, 16)

2. DEGREE WORDS

a. *Deletions*

> as ~~completely~~ sympathetic (PPU, 5)
> but ~~actually~~ of (SA, 6)
> ~~perfectly~~ sane children . . . perfectly sane adults (SA, 7)
> on ~~exactly~~ the same ground (SA, 7)
> ~~insincerely~~ Pharasaical (SA, 9)
> the ~~more~~ obvious conflicts (PPU, 2)

~~only~~ too liberally (PPU, 20)

the ~~purely~~ theoretical nature (PPU, 25)

b. *Additions*

simply as (PPU, 3)

a *very* modest banking account (PPU, 3)

far more puzzling (PPU, 20)

the *very* few managers (PPU, 21)

so disconcerting that (Rules, 4)

c. *Changes*

I am abundantly interested in both

I appreciate the value of both (PPU, 17)

    our most enlightened managers

    our more enlightened managers (PPU, 9)

Mr. Whistler and other really able artists

Mr. Whistler and his party (SA, 2)

    the most genial

    the more genial (PPU, 5)

a comparatively coarse kind of drama

the crude drama (PPU, 5)

    seem altogether unaccountable

    seem a wonder (PPU, 15)

a certain class of customers

very ordinary customers (PPU, 15)

    easier

    no harder (PPU, 16)

3. QUANTITY, EXTENT, INTENSITY, LIMITS, DEGREE

a. *Deletions*

he is ~~shallow and unfeeling enough to be~~ the dupe of . . . (SA, 6)

higher ~~than itself~~ (PPU, 6)

~~on the noblest works~~ of Mozart (PPU, 7)

had won ~~great~~ distinction (PPU, 9)

it set ~~hundreds of~~ clear-sighted students (SA, 2)

~~more or less~~ as a (SA, 5)

b. *Additions*
   to the full extent of my understanding of him (PPU, 5)
   ten times more (PPU, 23)
   unromantic (*but all the more dramatic*) facts (PPU, 23)
   In *all* these cases (Cen, 3)

c. *Changes*
   the critics
   many of my critics (PPU, 24)
       as a pure comedic entertainment
       hardly more than a bravura piece (PPU, 10)
   accepts a thousand rules for every one he challenges
   accepts a hundred rules for every one he challenges (SA, 5)
       better than Florence
       more hopeful than the Italian cities (PPU, 3)
   is playing a larger and larger part in
   is affecting . . . to an unprecedented extent (PPU, 16)
       that sum
       £1,700 (PPU, 2)
   until not the Church of England
   with such power that not the Church of England (PPU, 4)
       can hardly have been less than £4,000
       was not far from £5,000 (PPU, 2)
   to go forty miles with less labor than he used to go twenty
   to go twenty miles with less labor than he used to go seven
   (SA, 6)
   easier of access than most
   no harder of access than any (PPU, 16)
       his cleverest followers
       his disciples (SA, 2)
   for any dramatist
   for all qualified playwrights (PPU, 16)
       a certain class of
       great numbers of (PPU, 15)
   Chief among his tricks is the
   Take as a first specimen the (SA, 7)

great beauty
artistic beauty (PPU, 21)
in Candida
in the highest art (PPU, 22)

4. INTRODUCTORY "THAT"

   a. *Deletions*
   ~~still missing the fact that~~ (SA, 4)
   ~~The truth is that~~ passion (SA, 4)

   b. *Additions*
   without pretending that (PPU, 9)
   Just let me explain that when (SA, 6)
   I half expect that those managers (PPU, 21)
   the rest will . . . , *proving that* . . . , and *that* . . . (Rules, 5)

   c. *Changes*
   pretences of
   pretences that (PPU, 26)
   All these things can be humanized
   I was more than willing to shew that the drama can humanize
      these things (PPU, 12)

5. THE SERIES

   a. *Additions*
   kindness and truth and justice (SA, 4)
   the *Paris journalist, the* Dresden conductor, the designer and
      founder of the Bayreuth enterprise, the . . . , and the
      . . . (SA, 8)
   If a man's senses are acute, he is degenerate, hyperaesthesia
      having been observed in asylums. *If they are dull, he is
      degenerate, anaesthesia being the stigma of the craziness
      which made old women confess to witchcraft.* If he is
      particular . . . , he is degenerate . . . . If . . . . If . . . .
      If . . . ; if on the other hand . . . . If . . . ; if . . . ;
      if not . . . . (SA, 9)
   of destruction, *confusion,* and ruin (PPU, 20)

has been *romantic: that is spurious,* cheap and vulgar (PPU, 16)

without any actors ~~and~~ *critics, or* dramatists (PPU, 18)

of an inhuman and freakish wantonness, of *preoccupation with "the seamy side of life";* of paradox, cynicism, *and* eccentricity (PPU, 22)

progress, science, morals, *religion, patriotism,* imperial supremacy, national greatness, and all the other . . . (PPU, 26)

an incoherent, aimless, *formless,* endless meandering (SA, 3)

you have *legality,* duty, obedience, self-denial, submission to external authority (SA, 5)

And many more, both in these categories and in others such as proper names, references to propositions, all-or-nothing determiners, and so on. My impression is that out of all the brief revisions I examined, around half bear importantly on structural or semantic categories that Shaw favors throughout his prose. To repeat, these categories represent a small proportion of all conceivable ones, and the fact that they receive so much attention in his revisions encourages the supposition with which I began. This one reviser, at least, is particularly likely to alter his stylistic choices within areas of high epistemic sensitivity for him. The reader will have noticed, furthermore, that the revisions as a group neither greatly increase nor greatly diminish the number of especially Shavian locutions (the one exception is the Shavian series, which, like the national debt, always grows, never shrinks). Apparently Shaw's epistemic restlessness in these areas presses him, not to more and more idiosyncratic forms of expression, but merely to activity and change. The conclusion to be drawn is simply that these choices are the ones that matter to him, not that his decisions all make for stylistic extremity.

INDEX

Index

NOTE: This index does not include works of Shaw quoted in the text purely as examples of a stylistic feature, nor does it include names or subjects mentioned by Shaw in such quotations.